VOICES FROM THE BORDER

Response to Chinese Claims over Arunachal Pradesh

Editors

Gurudas Das

C Joshua Thomas

Nani Bath

PENTAGON PRESS

Voices from the Border: Response to Chinese Claims over Arunachal Pradesh
Gurudas Das, C Joshua Thomas and Nani Bath (Editors)

ISBN 978-81-8274-834-7

First Published in 2015

Published by
PENTAGON PRESS
206, Peacock Lane, Shahpur Jat,
New Delhi-110049
Phones: 011-64706243, 26491568
Telefax: 011-26490600
email: rajan@pentagonpress.in
website: www.pentagonpress.in

Branch
Flat No.213, Athena-2,
Clover Acropolis,
Viman Nagar,
Pune-411014
Email: pentagonpresspune@gmail.com

Printed at Aegean Offset Printers, Greater Noida

Contents

Preface

Territorial disputes have been the major cause of inter-state wars all along the human history. During the medieval period, while land was the main source of wealth, feudal states often used to follow the policy of territorial aggrandizement. As a result, territorial boundaries of feudal states were largely functions of political and military power of their governments. The territorial boundary of a feudal state used to expand or contract with the rise and fall of the state power within or across the dynasties. The idea of international boundary, in the modern sense of the term, between states, thus, could not emerge during the medieval period. Rather, the authority of the feudal states over territorial spaces was overlapping and shifting. This was more so in bordering areas which were either loosely administered or often left out of the ambit of regular administration.

Unlike Western nations where modern states, by and large, inherited the political boundaries created, negotiated and protected by their feudal predecessors, in large parts of Asia, Africa and Latin America, colonial powers mediated the graduation from feudal to modern state boundaries. On their independence, countries in these continents accepted and inherited the political boundaries set by the colonial powers through innumerable treaties, pacts and conventions.

Like the territorial boundary under feudal state that lacks precision due to its nature of being in constant flux, the same set by the colonial powers, in many a case, often lacks legitimacy as it was often thrust upon the neighbouring state(s), unless the previously delineated boundary is agreed upon and ratified by the modern states.

Sino-Indian border presents such a dilemma. While China contests the legitimacy of the colonial McMahon Line, India questions Chinese claim over territories based on feudal loyalty structure (area-under-Tibetan-influence hypothesis). Without any serious attempt to resolve the differences across the table, a war was fought between them in 1962 that had frozen their relationship for about three decades.

While it is being increasingly realized that a state can gain more through specialization and international trade, and development of economic interdependence (the present Sino-Indian trade volume stands as a pointer) than territorial expansion, adoption of a policy of territorial revisionism (for example, Chinese claim over Arunachal Pradesh) could ignite a major war leading to human sufferings and destruction. Moreover, as the militaristic and strategic significance of a border location has lost much relevance in the age of Inter Continental Ballistic Missile, 'the consent of the governed' principle is increasingly gaining currency among the international state system as the cardinal measure for the delineation of the inter-state boundaries. Thus, voice of the people living in the bordering regions must be factored into before making any territorial claims by the states in the international system.

It is in this context that a seminar on "Voices from the Border: India's Response to Chinese Claims over Arunachal Pradesh" was organized in Itanagar, the capital of the border state of Arunachal Pradesh, to deliberate upon the issue of Chinese claim over this state during March 8-9, 2012, where a cross section of people from academics, administration, civil society, diplomatic services, journalists, politicians and citizens took part and contributed to the discussions. The present volume is the product of these deliberations. The views and opinions expressed in this collection of essays are exclusively of the authors, and the editors have only facilitated their publication in order to place them in the public domain.

We are grateful to Professor D R Syiehmleih, Vice Chancellor, Rajiv Gandhi University, Itanagar, for hosting the seminar and providing all sorts of logistic support towards its successful completion. We are also grateful to General JJ Singh, Governor, Arunachal Pradesh, for showing keen interest on this subject and extending all possible support including delivering a brilliant inaugural address which could not be incorporated here for matters of protocol. We greatly appreciate Professor Mrinal Mri, Chancellor, Rajiv Gandhi University and Ambassador (Rtd) C V Ranganathan for their excellent presentation in the seminar. Professor Nani Bath, Department of Political Science, Rajiv Gandhi University, his colleagues and research scholars deserve special thanks for their kind cooperation in holding the event. We express our heartfelt gratitude to the Government of Arunachal Pradesh, Rajiv Gandhi University, the Indian Council of Social Science Research (ICSSR), New Delhi, and the ICSSR North Eastern Regional Centre for extending financial grants towards this seminar.

We are thankful to Mr Ujjwal Kanti Paul for providing secretarial assistance in the process of compilation of the contributions in the press-ready format.

Editors

Contributors

Akester, Matthew, Independent Scholar on Modern Tibetan Studies, trinsam@gmail.com

Basar, Gomar, Research Scholar, Centre for East Asian Studies, JNU, New Delhi, gomarkarko@gmail.com

Bath, Nani, Professor, Department of Political Science, Rajiv Gandhi University, Itanagar, Arunachal Pradesh

Bhaumik, Subir, Editor, Sever Sisters Daily, Guwahati, sbhaum@gmail.com

Das, Gurudas, Department of Humanities & Social Sciences, National Institute of Technology, Silchar, gurudas_das@yahoo.co.in

Goswami, Namrata, Research Fellow, Institute for Defence Studies and Analyses, New Delhi, namygoswami@gmail.com

Jacob, T Jabin, Assistant Director, Institute of Chinese Studies, Delhi, jabinjacob@gmail.com

Kondapalli, Srikanth, Professor in Chinese Studies & Chairman Centre for East Asian Studies, #141 School of International Studies, Jawaharlal Nehru University, New Delhi 110 067, srikondapalli@gmail.com

Mukherjee, John, Lt. Gen. (Retd), Vice President, CENERS-Kolkata, johnmukherjee@hotmail.com

Patnaik, Jajati, Associate Professor, Indira Gandhi Govt. College, Tezu, Arunachal Pradesh, pattnaik.jagoti61@gmail.com

Ranganathan, CV, Former Indian Ambassador to China, cvranganathan@gmail.com

Srikanth, H, Associate Professor, Dept of Political Science, North-Eastern Hill University, Shillong, hskant@gmail.com

Thomas, C. Joshua, Deputy Director, Indian Council of Social Science Research, North Eastern Regional Centre, Shillong, Meghalaya, cjoshuathomas@gmail.com

List of Tables and Maps

Chapter 1

Introduction

Much of the recent history of Sino-Indian bilateral relations is fraught with mutual distrust. Nehru-Zhou Enlai's "Hindi-Chini bhai bhai" has given way to "Hindi-Chini bye bye" following the 1962 border conflict. In spite of plethora of literature available on this issue, many questions are still left unanswered. Why did China launch the military campaign across the Himalayas in 1962? Was it because of India's "forward policy" in the Himalayas to catch up the McMahon Line, that she took as given as part of the British Indian Empire to which China had reservation? If this had been the reason, then why did China withdraw beyond that line without any negotiation? Does Chinese withdrawal mean her acceptance, *albeit* with dissent, of the McMahon Line? If that is the case, why did China wreck up the issue almost after four decades of silence by way of raising the shrill claim over Arunachal Pradesh, which used to be a buffer region, south of McMahon Line, between British India and Tibet?

While China has settled demarcation of her borders with other countries, why is she lengthening the process of settlement in case of Sino-Indian border? Is India's non-negotiable position, as perceived by the Chinese, in regard to McMahon Line standing on the way? Does not Chinese Line of Actual Control (LAC) approximate India's McMahon Line? If the answer is affirmative, then where is the problem in settling the border in the Eastern Sector? Why did China insist for a package deal like swapping the Aksai Chin in the Western Sector under Chinese control for Arunachal Pradesh in the Eastern Sector under Indian control? Does it mean that China seeks to legalize her occupation of Aksai Chin which she otherwise cannot justify? Is the Chinese assertion of claim over Arunachal Pradesh a maximalist ploy in response to India's strategy for sector-by-sector approach towards border negotiation?

Although India has officially accepted Chinese suzerainty over Tibet and has compromised with her loss of interest in Tibet, does India's patronage to Tibetan Government in Exile play the spoilsport in settling the border row? While the Kingdom of Tibet is dead, how does it benefit India in patronizing the Tibetan Government in Exile? By not settling the border issue, is not China keeping the Tibet issue alive so that it can play a Balkan in Asia with the unfolding of time? Why does the Tibet issue remain at the centre of Sino-Indian relations even after Chinese occupation of Tibet and India's recognition of the fact that Tibet is a part of China? By claiming Arunachal Pradesh as part of Tibet and hence a part of China, does the Chinese government intend to send a signal to Tibetan constituency in the world in general and China in particular that she can better serve their interests than India? Does the Chinese claim over Arunachal Pradesh essentially aim at getting back the Tawang Tract with the 332-year-old Galden Namgey Lhatse Monastery, popularly known as Tawang Monastery, the birth place of Sixth Dalai Lama, due to the religious and emotional attachments of the Tibetans to it? As the Tawang Monastery is often viewed as the existence of "free Tibet" by the Tibetans outside the Hans dominated China, does the Chinese think that by capturing the Tawang Monastery they would be able to earn legitimacy to rule over Tibet and the Tibetans? Is it that the Chinese claim over Tawang is a key to cement control over Tibet?

Is it that keeping the border issue alive a part of Chinese strategy to outcompete India in the regional and global power matrix? While both the nations look for peaceful rise, does China think that ensuring the same for itself and jeopardizing the peace in India through proxy war via Pakistan would maximize the growth dividend to China at the cost of India? Could India see the Chinese game to keep her (India) embroil in South Asia while she (China) leapfrogs into the global arena? Has this realization about Chinese India containment policy led her to tilt towards America's China containment game that, as perceived by China, has manifested in India-USA nuclear deal where USA has gone out of the way to help India getting NSG (Nuclear Supplier Group) waiver even in spite of not signing the NPT (Non-Proliferation Treaty)? Why is it that following the declaration of India-USA nuclear deal in 2005, China asserted her claim over Arunachal Pradesh in 2006 and subsequently hardened her position in 2007, by denying visa to an IAS officer hailing from Arunachal Pradesh, in 2009, by blocking an ADB loan for Arunachal Pradesh, protesting against the visit of Indian Prime Minister to the state and also objecting to the visit of Dalai Lama to the state, and in 2012, by denying visa to another defence official from and opposing the visit of Indian Defence Minister to this state ? Can one see the correlation between India-USA nuclear deal that took shape during 2005-08 and the increasing Chinese assertion of claim over Arunachal Pradesh? Does China intend to browbeat to keep India away from America?

Does China follow some sort of coercive diplomacy vis-à-vis India that has been manifested in her programme of development of huge military build-up in Tibet and creation of war waging capacity by way of construction of airfields, roadway, railways and other communication infrastructure like aperture terminal satellite stations and fibre-optic communication network along the Chinese side of the LAC in Tibet opposite to Arunachal Pradesh? Are not the Chinese build-up of conventional and strategic missile capabilities, and deployment of medium range ballistic missiles in Tibet India-centric? Has not Chinese military activism in Tibet compelled India to switch over from "scorched earth" policy—a policy of keeping the borders deliberately underdeveloped so that enemy forces cannot make any sweeping progress—to a "forward policy"—a policy of building infrastructure in the border areas for quick movement of forces and materials and increase in force and arms deployment ? Where are these two countries heading to?

Is the claim over Arunachal Pradesh indicative of the tip of the iceberg of a larger Chinese game plan of encirclement of India to root out the peer competition at the regional and global level? Does China see an emerging USA-India-Japan-South Korea-Vietnam-Indonesia alliance against her regional and global aspirations? Is China using her favourable power differential vis-à-vis India to deter her (India) from joining USA's China containment policy?

Is the military activism in Tibet only a deterrent posture? Or is it a real threat by which China seeks to weed out any possible obstacle towards her relentless pursuit of comprehensive national power as both the countries are destined to compete in each other's geo-political and geo-economic spaces in the world in general and Asia in particular? What would happen if India opts to leverage out of her strategic partnership with USA in order to modernize and enhance her military capability? Will there be war? If yes, limited or total? In view of nuclear holocaust, will China repeat 1962 to snub

India once again in order to assume her role as a global power? In case China exercises this option, can she remain a stable global power with hostile India at her backyard? Would not a slightest adventurism lead to mutual destruction and the Chinese aspiration to become the global power end before it begins?

Instead of viewing Sino-Indian relations from adversarial prism, can one see the immense benefit that would accrue to both the nations if they remain cooperative partners? Is not the bilateral trade between these two countries touched at USD 75.59 billion during 2011-12, making China the largest trade partner of India in spite of having border dispute between them? Is not the size of the mutual investment between them rising? Would not both the nations benefit by mobilizing their synergies for mutual growth and development? Could not China better manage Tibetan affairs by accommodating India's security sensitivities? Could not India better manage her north eastern peripheries by accommodating Chinese interest in LAC? While the pay off of cooperation is much larger than confrontation, why does the political leadership in both the countries pay heed to the advices of the security establishments?

It is thus important that both India and China leave the historical baggage behind and enter into negotiations based on pragmatic options. A compromise has to be struck in between the feudal and colonial territorial claims over the Himalayas.

Contributions in this volume have attempted to answer some of the issues raised in the foregoing paragraphs. As the contributors hail from diverse fields having different perceptions of the central theme of the volume, instead of a monolithic structure of argument, the volume contains an array of issues arising from the dynamics of Sino-Indian relations.

In Chapter 2, Indian Ambassador to China (Rtd), C V Ranganathan, has attempted to answer as to why, in spite of radical change in Sino-Indian bilateral relations, the boundary settlement issue continues to remain elusive. He observed that the problem is persisting because national perspectives diverge considerably on the demarcation of border between the two nations. While India feels that the border with China is well demarcated based on customs, traditions, history and geography *albeit* with minimal room for minor adjustments, China feels that earlier settlement is not acceptable and there is larger room for negotiation based on detail study of the actual situation on the ground. Besides this, the centrality of Tibet in Sino-Indian relations has also been analyzed. He argued that an opportunity for settlement of border dispute had been lost while China hinted to swap western sector for eastern sector due to Indian denial to such proposal. Subsequently, inculcation of ideology of nationalism in China and aggressive political opposition in India has reduced the space for any sort of territorial compromise for the resolution of the vexed border dispute between India and China. Hence, both the countries need to create a conducive internal environment to find a politically acceptable solution of this problem based on give and take principle.

In Chapter 3, Srikanth Kondapalli, one of the noted China Watchers in India, has focused on the Indian response to China's rise in the world in general and in Asia in particular. He has noted as to how shifts in Chinese position on India's Jammu and Kashmir—from "silence" during the 1950s, supporting the UN resolution for plebiscite during the 1960s, "status quoits" approach during the 1980s, and leveling J&K as a disputed territory by way of issuing staple visa to the Indian citizens from this state during 2000s—has led to a change in India's position on Tibet—recognizing it to be a part of China during 1950s and 1980s but consequently emphasizing more on the autonomy aspect and not agreeing to declare Tibet to be an "inalienable" and "historical" part as China wants her to do so. Kondapalli has explained as to how change in China's Asia policy is being matched by India's changing foreign policy architecture on the one hand and how the interplay of bilateral assessment is creating a space for accommodation of each other in a competitive global political and economic environment on the other. He has also observed as to how the dynamics of Sino-Indian relations has led to the emergence of new strategic partnership in global politics.

In Chapter 4, Gurudas Das, a social scientist from the northeastern region, has focused on the options that India can weigh while articulating her China policy in a fast changing global geo-political environment characterized by decline of USA as a global economic power, weakening of EU, rise of China, growing Sino-Russian alliance, shift in USA's engagement from Middle East to Asia-Pacific region, decline of Japan and rise of ASEAN. He has explained China's India policy as well as India's China policy in terms of both orthodox and reformist point of view. While the orthodox perspective is much influenced by the militaristic assessment which factors into concerns of a nation's security establishments and hence evaluates the motivation of others based on one's own security threats, the reformist perspective takes into account the pay off from cooperation arising out of mutual accommodation. The trajectory of China's India policy is characterized by shifts from a "friendly neighbor" during the 1950s to a "weak and irritating neighbor" during 1960s to 1980s and then to "rising Asian power" since 1990s. Similarly, India's China policy is characterized by shifts from "friendly neighbor" during the 1950s to "hostile neighbour" during 1960s to 1970s to "hostile rising power" during the 1980s and 1990s and then to "global power" since the beginning of the 21st century. In view of changing global power structure, Das has deduced that India can leverage from this and chart out her own path of national development by engaging China economically and USA politically. Integrating economic benefits from China and technological benefits from the West, India can emerge as a global power in the years to come. Once India emerges as a global power, she will have the strength to negotiate her border dispute with China on equal footing.

In Chapter 5, Jabin T. Jacob, one of the China Watchers in India, argues that while Arunachal Pradesh remains central to the boundary dispute, its significance for the two parties to the dispute has varied over time. For China, the shift in emphasis to Arunachal was in large measure tied to the Tibet question, and this emphasis has, if anything, become more important in recent years as instability and protests in Tibet have increased. He also argues that Arunachal ought to be seen in the Sino-Indian relationship not only within the context of the boundary dispute but also within the framework of centre-periphery relations in China and India and in the larger context of the differences between the Chinese and Indian political systems. The nature of Arunachal Pradesh's relations with the rest of India, including the Indian central government, is important not just for the Indian body politic but also for Sino-Indian relations and for Beijing's relations with Tibet.

In Chapter 6, Namrata Goswami, a security analyst, offers an analysis on the Chinese territorial claim on Arunachal Pradesh from the perspective of three significant factors. First, she looks within China's internal dynamics in order to determine the reasons propelling China's aggressive stand on Arunachal Pradesh. Secondly, she analyses the impact of the Tibet factor on China's aggressive posture. And finally, the play of international politics based on the "balance of power" in Asia vindicated by the rise of India and China is factored in to offer a framework to understand the current tensions. She observes that China's territorial claim on Arunachal Pradesh has great symbolic resonance for its legitimacy over Tibet. If Chinese regime stability is high and it manages its internal contradictions, then China will avoid doing anything seriously aggressive in Arunachal Pradesh. If Chinese regime stability is low, and its internal contradictions gets acute, then China will be aggressive with regard to Arunachal Pradesh to divert people's attention from internal instability. Nationalism will also be shored up in order to create the internal environment for right flat form for China's quest to occupy Arunachal Pradesh (what china calls as Southern Tibet). However, she feels that a Sino-Indian border dispute is not intractable. This has to be resolved within a policy of "give and take". Too much of rigid posturing by both sides will create obstacles. The 2005 framework agreement between India and China offers a broad outline within which the border issue can be resolved.

In Chapter 7, Gomar Basar, an Arunachalee scholar, has traced the evolution of inner line in the Eastern Himalayas during the colonial period which China considers as the boundary of British India and claims the unadministered territory, comprising the present Indian state of Arunachal Pradesh, as part of Tibet by default overlooking the British idea of nebulous outer line. Basar provides the glimpse of historical account of Qing dynasty's attempt to invade Tibet in 1910 and subsequent declaration of independence by Tibet following the abdication of Qing emperor in 1911. Although not recognized by China, British signed the *Simla Accord* with this "independent Tibet" in order to delineate McMahon Line as a boundary between British India and Tibet which provides the raison d'être for the Indian claim. However, as the McMahon Line, which has been drawn only on map at a scale 1:38,00,000, a one-degree variation on the map involves several miles variation on the ground. As a result, misperception of the line on the ground leads to intrusion into each other's perceived territory. Moreover, it is difficult for China to accept the McMahon Line as a border with India because the acceptance of the line would tantamount to recognizing Tibet as an independent country leading to China's self-admission of the fact that Tibet has been occupied, which diametrically opposes Chinese official position vis-à-vis Tibet.

In Chapter 8, J R Mukherjee, a retired colonel in Indian Army who had the privilege to serve along the McMahon Line, articulates in encapsulate form the claims and counterclaims over Arunachal Pradesh by China, Tibetan movement for autonomy, and India. He details out the rationale for Chinese claims over areas south of McMahon line and the counterclaims by India. He observes, as far as the Eastern Sector is concerned, that Chinese claim arises from: (a) different perceptions about the McMahon Line on the ground, and (b) perceived historical, theological and civilizational influences of Tibet across the McMahon Line. He analyzes the nature of territorial disputes on the ground along the LAC and the strategic implications of Chinese specific territorial claims for India. He observes that India's position on Tibet and the Tibetan movement for autonomy has been at the root of China's renewed assertion of her claim over Arunachal Pradesh. A review of Indian approach to Tibetan affairs would go a long way towards the resolution of the vexed Sino-Indian border dispute in the Eastern Sector.

In Chapter 9, Mathew Alkester, a scholar on Tibetan Affairs, reviews the history of Tibet's relations with what is now the Indian state of Arunachal Pradesh, what the Tibetans used to call "Loyul" meaning the 'land of the Lopa'. Using evidences from micro-history prior to the Chinese occupation of Tibet, the author exhibits that apart from one small exception involving the Pachakshiri enclave, now known as Mechuka, in West Siang, a valley colonized by Tibetans apparently from the early 18th century, Ganden Potrang (Tibetan state) had no powers of administration or taxation in Loyul south of the McMahon line. As a result, China's claim over Arunachal Pradesh being part of Tibet stands out to be ahistorical.

In Chapter 10, Subir Bhaumik, one of the veteran journalists who hails from the northeastern region, narrates the renewed Chinese interest in providing logistic support to the insurgent groups of northeast India. He makes a conjecture that this effort might be interpreted as one of the set of other initiatives that have been initiated as part of its counter-strategy against India's stepping into the US strategy to encirclement of China.

In Chapter 11, H. Srikanth, a political scientist of northeastern region, has made a critic against the uncritical acceptance of international borders by the post-colonial states that were drawn by the colonial powers. He favours a negotiated settlement for the resolution of the Sino-Indian border dispute rather than clinging to any pre-conceived notion of colonial border. He argues in favour of the much talked about swap between western and eastern sectors as a viable option for dispute settlement as it would be feasible to evolve national consensus in both the countries on this line.

In Chapter 12, Jajati K Pattnaik, a scholar from northeastern region, argues in favour of Sino-Indian cooperation and mobilization of synergies across the border for the common good of the people of both the countries. He enumerates the elements of "soft power" in both India and China and asserts that their combined strengths have the capacity to lead the world besides portraying as to how bilateral cooperation could make the tool of cross-border trade more effective that can address the problem of development of the frontier regions in both the nations. He observes that the recent developments in Sino-Indian relations particularly the earnest attempts from both sides to arrive at a solution to the vexed border issue do not fit into the repeated Chinese claim over Arunachal Pradesh. He cautions that the issue involving Arunachal Pradesh should not be allowed to hijack in realizing the dream of the great Chinese leader Deng Xiaoping in making the 21st century an Asian Century, which would be possible only through mutual accommodation of each other by both the nations.

In Chapter 13, C. Joshua Thomas, a political scientist of the north eastern region, argued for cooperative relationship between India and China rather than adversarial relationship. As the confrontational politics is going to yield negative dividend for both since none of them has undisputable historical evidence behind their claim over Arunachal Pradesh and nationalist interpretations of history do not converge, it is prudent for both the nations to settle the boundary dispute in the Eastern Sector along the Line of Actual Control. A coercive border policy, as China appears to have been pursuing, might lead to nuclear holocaust in the Asian continent. Instead, a cooperative relationship by way of mutual accommodation of each other's interest would be a win-win situation for both.

The central point of discourse in this volume is the assertion of China's claim over Arunachal Pradesh in recent times and to understand the politics of "territorial claim" as a bargaining strategy that China is playing to obfuscate the US stratagem of containment of China in which, it feels, India is getting embroiled. The lion's share of the contributions that have gone in the making of this volume have come from the people residing in the Northeastern region. A number of contributions have also been added from the people residing in the state of Arunachal Pradesh. The idea is to bring the voices from the border out on an issue which is being claimed and counterclaimed by the two nation states in Asia. Much of the contributions from scholars, having diverse disciplinary backgrounds, belong to the academic domain of strategic studies. In the event of the absence of any authentic historical evidences from either side, a consensus has emerged in favour of negotiated settlement of the border dispute between India and China based on "give and take" spirit.

Shillong **Editors**
April 15, 2015

Chapter 2

Enduring India-China Boundary Question: Changing India-China Relations and Geopolitical Situation

C.V. Ranganathan

The title of this volume *Voices from the Border: Response to Chinese Claims on Arunachal Pradesh* is both appropriate and timely. Timely because the India-China boundary question needs to be revisited in an attempt to answer two paradoxes: The question has endured in spite of vast changes for the better in India-China bilateral relations; the question has endured in spite of vast changes in the geopolitical situation. This has, by and large, been beneficial to both India and China in recent decades, far removed from 1962 when the armed conflict took place. My effort is to seek personal answers to these two paradoxes. Logically speaking, the maturity displayed by both Governments of India and China to constantly drive the vast improvements in bilateral relations between these two countries and a geopolitical context where the ambitions and entitlements of both India and China have grown and acknowledged by the world at large, could have led to solutions to the huge differences between the two on the extent of each side's territorial jurisdiction. That such a thing has not happened is at least partly to be explained by certain political and social circumstances which have emerged in both the countries. These show some continuities with the past when the conflict took place.

Correspondence at the levels of the Premiers in 1959 on the boundary question showed the wide differences between the two Governments in their respective approaches to the question. India's approach was that the India-China boundary was well settled as it was based on customs, traditions and history. It was sanctified by imposing geographical features as well as agreements and treaties for most parts of the boundary. Minor adjustments were however possible in arriving at a solution. The Chinese approach on the other hand was that with the establishment of the People's Republic of China, the new Government would make studies on China's borders with neighbors since many of these were drawn in earlier historical periods. After such studies, the Government would be prepared for negotiations to settle the boundaries on the basis of mutual understanding and mutual accommodation. The three years between 1959 and 1962 were characterized by misunderstandings, misperceptions and even lost opportunities for a negotiated settlement acceptable to both the sides. These, in turn, arose from the domestic circumstances which prevailed in both the countries as well as from certain factors external to both the countries.

The centrality of the role of Tibet after the entry of People's Liberation Army in 1950, and later in 1959 when His Holiness Dalai Lama sought refuge in India, has been emphasized often enough. In 1950, India's note to the Chinese Government to seek a peaceful solution to China's relations with Tibet was seen as interference in a domestic matter. An authoritative article in the official media, People's Daily, accused Premier Nehru of following the British Imperialist policies relating to Tibet. This erroneous perception got worsened in 1959 after Dalai Lama came to India when most intemperate accusations were made by the Chinese that India had instigated his escape from Lhasa and that India had not reconciled to China exercising its authority over Tibet. In spite of India and Tibet signing the 1954 Agreement on Trade and Intercourse between India and the Tibet Autonomous Region, where India recognized Chinese sovereignty over Tibet, China under Mao Zedong's leadership did not accept the distinction made in India's stand. This was to accept Tibet as a part of China while offering humanitarian asylum to the Dalai Lama and his followers in accordance with well accepted international norms. The reference by China to India's Arunachal Pradesh as "Southern Tibet" over recent years continues its focus on Tibet and we will turn to this aspect later.

From the mid-fifties, a contributory factor to the 1962 conflict and worsening India-China relations after that was the complete misunderstanding by the Chinese leadership of the Indian Parliamentary system and its free

Press. Chinese actions in expanding their occupation in Ladakh Sector, treatment of an Indian Patrol Party in that sector by the Chinese soldiers before they were released in 1959, Dalai Lama's refuge in India and the publication of inter-governmental correspondence on the boundary and other matters, combined to inflame public opinion in India. This had, in turn, severely narrowed Prime Minister Nehru's room for negotiations relating to the boundary in 1960 when Premier Zhou Enlai visited India. He requested Nehru to "take a view on the Western Sector (Ladakh) similar to that taken by China in case of the Eastern Sector". The same thought was reproduced when Deng Xiaoping met A.B. Vajpayee who visited China as an External Affairs Minister in 1979. On both the occasions, Indian leadership's response was altogether negative, wherein as the exchange of territory implicit in the proposal was unacceptable. On both occasions, a strong opposition from the political parties and from the senior leaders within parties played a pivotal role in causing lost opportunities to approach a settlement of the boundary question.

A major external factor contributing to China's calculations with regard to relations with India was also the rapidly deteriorating state of Party and State level relations between it and the former Soviet Union (FSU). Its origin can be traced to Mao Zedong's intolerance for what he saw as FSU's hegemonistic behavior and his own hyper nationalistic view of China's place in the world as a revolutionary force. The evolution of friendly relations between Kruschev-led FSU and India and his initiatives to reconcile with U.S.A were seen as a betrayal by FSU of socialist solidarity. The latter's apparently neutral call for negotiations between India and China after the armed incident in Longju in 1959 and its expression of regret at the loss of life was denounced as being partial to a non-socialist country (India) instead of supporting a socialist one (China). At a meeting between Mao and Kruschev in 1959 at Beijing, the latter deemed Nehru to be progressive, that China's actions towards India would bring setbacks to the cause of socialism, and that peaceful negotiations should be undertaken by China with India. Although such negotiations did take place in 1960 when Zhou Enlai visited India, the 1962 armed conflict with India is seen, by academicians in retrospect, as a punitive mission aimed at the FSU as much as it was directed against India, albeit long after the event. Through the mid-sixties, when the Great Proletarian Cultural Revolution was launched by Mao and which lasted till his death in 1976, relations between FSU and China worsened, even as

India's relations with it grew to include political and military cooperation. The Chinese leadership view then was that India was not non-aligned, but that it was doubly aligned both to FSU and USA. Such misperceptions about India's domestic and external policies persisted almost to the late seventies. Reforms were initiated by Deng Xiaoping with regard to China's domestic policies and also to its external policies which were aimed at working for a peaceful neighborhood surrounding China. India, like other South East neighbors of China, benefitted from these great changes as indeed did the Chinese people. In fact such has been the spectacular economic growth and its translation to military might over the last four decades that after the Western economic failures since the first decade of this century, the world looks at China with heightened expectation that it would play a far bigger and more responsible role in bringing more equilibrium in the world's political, security and economic order.

Failures on the part of the civil and military leaderships in India, erroneous assessments of the evolving ground positions along the boundary, a misplaced confidence that the wide differences would not lead to a full scale attack by the Chinese army and that an armed conflict would inevitably involve intervention by the big powers, have all been commented upon and written about by Indian and foreign writers and perhaps need no repetition here. Sixty years after the 1962 conflict both India and China reflecting their considerable economic achievements have also modernized their armed forces to a considerable extent. India's armed forces in striking contrast to the sixties have the self-confidence that they are capable of defending the borders even as bilateral relations between India and China have improved vastly, encompassing many diverse fields. These include a web of agreements which ensure the maintenance of peace and tranquility along the India-China boundary, which has seen no armed actions over recent decades. Expertise has been developed enabling India to manage the boundary situation despite each side having different perceptions of the Line of Actual Control separating the two sides' armed forces. The status quo on the ground since 1962 has prevailed and successfully defended by India. However, Chinese reiterations that Arunachal Pradesh constitutes China's "Southern Tibet" in more recent pronouncements only add to the deep lack of trust which exists in India since 1962 about China. On the other hand it also fuels Chinese nationalism which view all of Chinese claims, land and maritime as legitimate and non-negotiable.

As for a permanent solution to the boundary question it has been publicly acknowledged by the leadership of both countries that it would take much more time to resolve even as they are committed not to allow the existence of the question to impede the growth of relations in all possible fields. Over several rounds of dialogue, Special Representatives appointed by the Premiers to examine it, both sides have reached the second stage of a three-stage process of agreeing on political principles which should guide a solution and a framework leading to the last stage of a solution agreeable to both sides.

Turning to the geopolitical situation in Asia at present, from the beginning of the 21st century, India's relations with the major powers, USA, Russia, Japan, China, Brazil and with the major regional groupings, European Union, Association of South Eastern Nations, Brazil-Russia-India-China-South Africa grouping and many others have seen significant improvements. By virtue of its size, geography, economic and social achievements and the accretion of its military strength including nuclear capability, India is perceived as a valuable partner with the potential to play constructive roles to ensure regional peace and stability and participate effectively in dialogues on subjects on the international agenda. The growth of the Indian Navy is perceived as an important asset in the maintenance of peace in a vast oceanic space from the Western to the Eastern Indian Ocean. The humanitarian role played by the Navy in times of natural disasters has been welcomed. The acceptance of the Indian Navy as a factor for peace and stability has obvious political and security implications particularly for Asia. India is expected to play a role in the fashioning of a multilateral architecture for South East and East Asia.

This beneficial change in the geopolitical situation in India's favor needs to be worked upon by India, in such a manner as both exercising and seen to be exercising its traditional sense of strategic autonomy and pursuing its national interests. In the case of China, the geopolitical situation in Asia poses new challenges, which it did not have to countenance to the same extent before a few years. Its aggressive behavior towards Japan, Republic of Korea and some South East Asian countries revolving around disputes over maritime claims has strengthened the hedging actions taken by China's neighbors to consolidate their military relations with USA, thus to ensure America's continued political and security involvement in Asia. In view of the end games in Iraq and Afghanistan the USA has also made a policy determination to "pivot" to Asia from 2012. This involves the enhancing of its military commitments to Asian neighbors of China.

The world at large is facing a China which is excessively preoccupied with a long held stability-security syndrome. In a year of transition of the top leadership the effects of this syndrome are more evident. In domestic affairs the language used by Premier Wen Jiabao to describe problems confronting China emphasizes multiple crises: restructuring an economy which was export dependent, reducing the roles of the state sector in public investments, raising domestic demand, meeting energy conservation targets, reducing regional disparities and the rich-poor divide, and so on. A bigger social and political challenge is to institute credible political reforms to the one-party governance system in an era of heightened expectations which find public articulations in the Internet space. The Communist Party membership has reached 80, 000 and ensuring that arbitrary, illegal and immoral actions by some Party cadres do not take place is a problem. The elimination of deep-rooted corruption is seen as a life and death struggle by the leadership. Public dissatisfaction often gives place to demonstrations, even riots and destruction of property.

In a vast territorial area inhabited by minorities in Tibet and Xinjiang, there is increasing restiveness. There are strong perceptions that the fruits of development in Tibet and Xinjiang are enjoyed by the immigrant Han communities at the cost of the minorities. The Chinese are confronted by the reality that progress, higher incomes and development for the minorities in these regions do not eliminate the deep urge to have social, religious, cultural identities given more respect than given at present. Deep feelings of alienation among the minorities may also have an influence on delicate issues such as territorial concessions which are necessary if the boundary question with India is to be resolved to the mutual satisfaction of the peoples of India and China. The scale of the threat perception to stability both in China proper and in Tibet and Xinjiang can be gauged by the decision of the leadership to allocate a bigger budget to public security forces than to the regular defense forces in the last meeting of the Parliament. In this background, it is not expected that the new Party leadership which may be in place in 2012 will take political steps matching economic growth to meet the aspirations of people for change.

Complementing the emphasis on domestic stability is the perceptions of external threats to China's security. The unfortunate happenings in Provinces of China where Tibetans reside, such as self-immolations of lamas are seen as instigated by Dalai Lama and his followers. Maritime activity by neighboring countries in accordance with international norms is sometimes seen as violation of Chinese sovereignty over these areas thus challenging acknowledged practices. The rapid growth of Indo-USA, Indo-Japan and Indo-Korean relations, including in the political, security and military spheres are seen as undisguised attempts at containing China. In viewing with apprehension India's relations with USA, the Chinese may unwittingly revert to an earlier era, when as pointed out earlier, there was no proper appreciation of the essence of India's foreign policy, respected by all political parties, which is to maintain strategic autonomy. As stated by India's Prime Minister on occasions India does not seek to use its evolving relationship with USA against China. In the case of USA too the deep stake in its interdependence with China is a positive restraint on attempts at trying to contain it.

Reverting to what was said at the beginning on continuities with the troubled period of India-China relations, resolution of the boundary question can only come about on a basis of give and take and each side making territorial adjustments. For this to succeed both governments must make assiduous efforts to bridge a big gap in public perceptions of the India-China relationship, which is sound. However, the existing asymmetry between governments and opinion makers in both countries is very wide and not conducive to arriving at an acceptable consensus on the boundary. In India coalition governance and confrontational opposition party conduct make consensus seeking difficult. In China the cultivation of nationalistic feelings as a substitute for socialist ideology and the problems in Tibet where the regime feels insecure seem to work against early territorial compromise. As for factors external to India-China relations, such as the scope and content of Indo-USA relations, it would be an excellent initiative if tripartite dialogues at official levels between India-China-USA are held to remove distrust and seek approaches to ensuring peace and stability in regions where the interests of all three are heavily involved. A good example of such a region is the area referred to as Af-Pak by the Americans. Here the interests of all three to see the reemergence of a stable, moderate and modernizing Afghanistan, free from foreign interference, coincide. The tripartite dialogue can also include major items on the international agenda.

In conclusion what are the implications for the people of Arunachal Pradesh in all this? Although not covered in any detail, the scope, content and quality of relations developed between India and China in the last two decades precludes repetitions of 1962. Sufficient vested interests in the sturdy maintenance of peace and tranquility along the boundary have come into existence, both with Governments and the armed forces of both sides. It was heartening to note from the papers that there was overwhelming opinion in favor of reasoned dialogues to solve all outstanding questions between India and China. Sometimes single unverified reported "events" turn into symbols and these in turn develop their own momentum. The case of the waters flowing into India from Tibet is an example. This issue is one which involves India and Bangladesh and no unilateral actions can be taken to prevent the usual flows. The Indian and Chinese Governments have dialogue mechanisms to consider this question and obtain assurances. We will need to study the impending political changes in China to get a clearer picture of the next directions of India-China relations.

Chapter 3

Enough Space in Asia: Indian Responses to China's Rise

Srikanth Kondapalli

Introduction

China's strategic rise over the last three decades is leading to major changes in the international and regional environment. The global power structure—with the United Nations, Bretton Woods institutions, G-8/G-20 alliances and others—is now subjected to increasing influence of China. At the regional level, China has become the largest trading partner for several countries of Asia including India. It has recently proposed free trade areas or currency swap arrangements with many a country in the region. China also has been practicing varied policies in Asia—some accommodating and some posing direct or indirect challenges to other regional powers based on sovereignty issues or issues of power. At the South Asian level, China, while cobbling up a "strategic partnership and cooperation" with India in 2005, has been strengthening its position in Islamabad, Dhaka, Kathmandu and Colombo. China's role in the Indian Ocean Region is also increasing, partly in view of its energy and investment interests. In the light of the above developments, in addition to challenges in the maritime, cyber and space domains, Indian responses have been diverse—with self-help measures of protecting its sovereignty interests in regard to Kashmir and unresolved territorial disputes and partial band-wagoning with the United States, exploring comprehensive economic partnerships with Japan, South Korea, Southeast Asian states and the like.

India has been watching with keen interest and concern the strategic rise of China over the last three decades. As two large countries in Asia with the largest population in the world aiming to improve their livelihoods, economic conditions, and conventional and strategic military capabilities for projection of power, India and China have been adopting policies aimed at protecting and furthering their respective national interests, sovereignty and territorial integrity and jockeying for great power status in the regional and international fora.

In the process, both see each other's action as reinforcing their respective economic and political interests in the international institutions and also compete for influence. Both have, nevertheless, avoided explicit conflict on a number of issues at the regional and international levels citing that there exists "Enough space in Asia and beyond" for both in pursuing their goals.[1] This paper looks at India's responses to China's rise and its impact at three levels—South Asia, bilateral and multilateral—over the recent decades and argues that the formulation of "Enough space in Asia", although transitory in nature, provides for stability in the bilateral relations in the short to medium term while depending on the global and regional power transition in the long term.

China's posture towards South Asia and India's responses

As a result of the rise of China, its policies towards South Asia are undergoing major transformations. China has revamped its "good neighbourliness" policy in the recent period as the political leadership decided to stabilize its economic development in the periphery in the event of any challenge to the country's security from the peripheries and also for mutual benefit.[2] As a result of this policy, China has expanded multipronged contacts with the neighbouring states, including those in South Asia.

China's relations with the South Asian countries are rooted in history, though the current state-to-state relations have emphasised aspects of territorial boundaries, sovereignty issues, trade and non-traditional security issues, given the geographical proximity of most of these countries to the politically sensitive ethnic regions of China. While during the Cold War, China followed a policy of building close relations with Pakistan, currently new policies are being implemented towards South Asia. In the fast changing international security environment in the wake of the collapse of the Soviet Union and the spread of the US influence in Central and South Asian region, China's western flank, specifically in Tibet and Xinjiang, it is assumed, would might face security problems.[3]

Stabilising its peripheries with the recently launched Western Development Campaign of opening the 16 provinces with infrastructure projects, coming to grip with rising India, nuclear stability in the region, counter-terrorism measures, exploration of markets for its burgeoning exports, raw material imports and exploring ways to secure sea lanes in the Indian Ocean for sustainable supplies of fuel to its economy—characterise the new features of China's interactions with the South Asian region in the recent period.

Towards India, Chinese strategic assessments categorise it as an "important country in South Asia". While this assessment is not yet passé, the US re-assessments in February 2005 on India to "help it to become a major power in the 21st Century" combined with enhancement in Indian comprehensive national strength are forcing China to re-assess its traditional policies.[4] India's higher economic growth rates, expanding information technology capabilities, military modernisation, etc. are said to be part of the recent Chinese reassessments on India.

Notwithstanding, one of the contentious issues between the two countries revolves around the status of Kashmir and Tibet. China's position on Kashmir has changed considerably over a period of time.[5] While the growing bonhomie between India and China during the 1950s witnessed a relative silence on the part of China, tensions between the two following the Dalai Lama's flight to India in 1959 and the subsequent border skirmish between the two countries led China to voice support in favour of the United Nations resolution calling for plebiscite in Kashmir Valley and for the right of the Kashmiris for self-determination. By the 1980s, China's position on the issue has considerably changed towards a *status quoist* position, partly due to the pragmatic leadership, growing influence of "separatism" by Uyghurs in Xinjiang, etc. Currently, China argues that the Kashmir dispute should be resolved peacefully between India and Pakistan, that neither of these countries should cross the line of control and that both should abide by the bilateral treaties.[6] Nevertheless, China has revised her Kashmir policy in terms of the Northern Areas and Pakistan occupied Kashmir as parts of Pakistan in 2009 and has issued stapled visas to Kashmiris in the Indian controlled areas. After diplomatic opposition from India, this position had been again revised in late 2010.

Similarly on Tibet, the Indian government has exhibited flexibility in 1954, 1988 and recently in June 2003 when it recognised Tibet as a part of China, although the recent position emphasises on the "autonomy" aspect of Tibet, while China insisted on India agreeing Tibet as an "inalienable" and "historical" part of China, which is not agreed upon so far. With Tibetan resistance and protests increasing in Tibet and abroad during the events leading to Beijing Olympics in 2008 and subsequently the above 80 self-immolation deaths of Tibetan monks by November 2012, indicated that the Indo-Tibetan regions are likely to remain one of the main areas of contention between China and the countries in the region.

Another feature of China's policy towards this region focuses on the strengthening of the Western China development campaign. For this, as India had been stalling any major economic engagement through borders, it is necessary for China to address the boundary dispute with India.[7] Although, eight talks were held during 1981-87 and 15 rounds during 1988-2005 under the Joint Working Group framework and 15 talks under the Special Representative level during 2003-12, there has been no major indication that this vexed issue could be resolved in near future. While three border passes have been opened up from 1993 to 2006, no major border trade passes through these lands. Nor is the number of trading items substantially increased through these border posts. While maritime trade is growing, with bilateral trade touching $25 billion in 2006 and $72 billion in 2011, India has been reluctant to sign a free trade area (FTA) with China, as it is concerned about Chinese dumping of goods, higher transportation and insurance charges, etc., although China's project investments have increased in India specifically in the energy and telecommunication sectors. India is also wary about China's ministry of water resource's plan to build huge hydro-electricity dams at Mutuo and Daduqiao at the Great Bend of Yarlong Zangbo— Brahmaputra River. These projects are estimated to be completed by 2050 with reports about diverting or constructing run of the river projects. India and Bangladesh as lower riparian states have concern over these projects. For instance, on June 11, 2000, Arunachal Pradesh experienced a disastrous flash flood. Himachal Pradesh as well had reported flash floods destroying apple cultivation in the region.[8]

In relation to Pakistan, although China maintains an "all-weather" friendship as reflected in enhanced political, diplomatic and military visits as compared to any other South Asian states, in the recent past, due to the killing of several Chinese in Pakistan, serious concerns are rising on possible linkage between Al Qaeda and the Uighur separatist movement in Xinjiang.[9] With this in view, China has conducted counter-terrorism exercises with Pakistan in August 2004 at Taxkorgan area, west of Tibet, at Pak-Afghan borders at Abbotabad in December 2006, at Ningxia, "friendship 2010" and other places, besides participating in the bilateral October 2003 Shanghai naval search and rescue operations and a multilateral naval exercise in the Arabian Sea in March 2007. China has also signed an FTA with Pakistan in November 2006. One of the prime considerations of Beijing during the Cold War period is to balance India by supporting Pakistan, specifically as India was seen as a large country in South Asia with the potential to challenge China.[10] While under Jiang Zemin and Hu Jintao's leaderships, Beijing had amended its position—specifically in the light of the spread of Uighur separatism and its connection to Pakistan, nevertheless, balancing India remained a prime consideration. This is reflected not only in the robust cooperation between Beijing and Islamabad in the conventional and strategic weapon platforms and systems and in supporting Pakistan's case for expanding its nuclear power (as reflected in its move at Nuclear Supplies Group on Chashma 3 and 4 plants in 2010)[11] but also in the close coordination in the diplomatic fields as well as on selective counter-terrorism efforts. China's plans for establishing bases abroad, specifically in the Indian Ocean Region, could also have larger consequences to the regional order—a factor that India is concerned with.[12] While India could hardly exert pressure on Beijing in the latter's cooperation with Pakistan, India had been able to exert persuasion and inserted a phrase in the joint declarations that the security concerns of each other (India and China) should be respected.

While China opposed the creation of Bangladesh in 1971, their post-1975 relations were cordial and expanding, specifically in political, military and energy fields. China eyes a large portion of the potential 60 trillion cubic feet of natural gas that Bangladesh possesses. Indeed, the Bangladeshi government has granted exploration rights to China and Begum Zia has invited China, during her visit to Beijing in August 2005, to develop gas fields. China is currently exploring gas explorations and possible construction of gas pipelines. Construction of a 1,250-kilometer pipeline from gas fields in Myanmar to its Yunnan province is being considered. This may be connected with Bangladesh in future. Reports indicate to the Chinese interest in acquiring container port facility at Chittagong and other military facilities in Bangladesh. Also, the Kunming-Chittagong road through Myanmar is under negotiation. Besides, China is exploring the first coal mine and constructing the coal-based power plant in Barapukuria, Bangladesh and, in November 2005, the first 125×2MW power plant was put into production. China built the Bangladesh-China Commercial Town with 500 Chinese shops at Kanchpur at a cost of about $6 million. This would further give a boost to the entry of Chinese goods into Bangladesh. China agreed to set up a nuclear power plant at Ropar in Bangladesh and has admitted Bangladesh, along with Pakistan, into the Chinese-led Asia-Pacific Space Cooperation Organisation in Beijing. Through these, Bangladesh is entitled to receive cooperation in nuclear and space technologies.

China's foreign policy objectives vis-à-vis Nepal is several. At a minimum, these objectives emphasise the security of Chinese interests in Tibet as that region is dependent on the neighbouring countries for border trade. Additionally, given the regular flow of thousands of Tibetan refugees into Nepal and India every year, Chinese objectives emphasise on nullifying any negative fallout of Tibetan refugees from these countries. Related to this objective is Chinese measure to counter the spread of Maoists influence in Nepal. This factor has assumed significance in the recent period as Nepalese Maoists have increased their influence in more than two-thirds of Nepalese territory. For China, if Maoists succeed in capturing state power in Kathmandu, there is always a prospect of increasing Maoist influence not only in other parts of China but also in Tibet. China offered nearly $13.7 million worth of small arms supply to Nepal to aid the Royal Nepalese Army's fight against the Maoists in 2005. China has extended cooperation to Nepal in terms of aid in constructing several highways including the Kathmandu-Lhasa route, leather factories, textiles, paper mills, sugar factories and other such projects. However, the assistance to the Lumbini project had run into rough weather. The total trade volume between China and Nepal is miniscule, although within this China enjoys a favourable balance of trade position.[13] In March 2006, visiting state councillor Tang Jiaxuan agreed to bridge the unfavourable trade by agreeing to provide duty free treatment to about 1,550 Nepalese goods export to China. Reports indicate that China is also planning to expand the Tibet railway into Nepal.

To cap these engagements with South Asia, China has expressed its desire to be part of the SAARC. At the 13th SAARC summit at Dhaka in 2005 China's candidature for observer position was accepted reportedly under Bangladesh, Pakistan and Nepal's pressure, while India wanted China first to sign bilateral MoUs with respective South Asian countries. Nevertheless, by 2007, China joined the SAARC as an observer at the 14th summit meeting at New Delhi but with the caveat that Afghanistan became a member, while Japan and others also become observers. This appeared to be a *quid pro quo* to the Chinese opposition to Indian candidature in the East Asian Summit, in which finally, under the pressure of Japan and Singapore India was admitted in 2005.

Bilateral Relations and Indian Responses

India had been carefully evaluating and responding to the strategic rise of China.[14] As recounted above, China had revamped its South Asia policy and had been engaging, in different intensities, with the South Asian states. This had resulted in fresh inputs in Indian responses. With its basic foreign policy postures of protecting sovereignty and territorial integrity, keeping a stable periphery and countering terrorism, enhancing economic development and maintaining strategic autonomy, Indian responses to China have exhibited a multi-pronged approach. These include enhancing cooperation at regional and international levels for mutual benefit with China, dissuading China from export of weapons of mass destruction to Pakistan, measures to enhance border stability, improving relations with the US, European Union, Russia, Japan and South Korea so as to enhance India's material capabilities, and the like.

Firstly, to usher in border stability, India had tied down China in mutually acceptable positions in resolving the territorial dispute, confidence building measures, prevent conditions that could trigger conflict, enhance conventional and strategic military capabilities in the event of any deterioration in relations, increase trade and investment profiles, expand people-to-people contacts, and the like. An agreement on the political parameters and guiding principles for the settlement of the boundary question was signed in 2005. Several CBMs were announced and practiced since 1978, but intensively in the 1990s. Officials on either side attended the first meeting of Joint Mechanism on Border Stability at Beijing in January 2012 after the idea was mooted a day before the BRICS summit meeting in 2011 at Sanya in China.

Secondly, a plethora of initiatives were launched in the economic sphere. This is in the backdrop of China's western development campaign of infrastructure development in its 16 western provinces and their links with the South, Central and Southeast Asian regions. These initiatives also intended to expand China's trade and interdependence and its influence in the South, Central and Southeast Asian region.[15] India had expanded trade contacts with a series of agreements and by 2011 bilateral trade increased to over $72 billion, although this is heavily in favour of China. Trade imbalance issues were raised by the high level leaders including the then President Patil and Prime Minister Manmohan Singh and others. Issues related to discrimination of the Indian software and pharmaceutical companies in China's market, low level of investments in the Indian market from China, etc. have come to the fore in the last few years.[16] Two strategic and economic dialogues were conducted between the two countries to arrive at a macro-economic perspective and for mutual benefit, specifically in the light of the global financial crisis and intensifying Euro Zone crisis. India had also expanded contacts with Japan, South Korea with which it had signed comprehensive economic partnership, and had signed a free trade agreement with the Southeast Asian countries and planning to have a similar agreement with Taiwan. These are intended to be a cushion against China's inroads as well as getting connected to the high growth regions.

Thirdly, in the backdrop of China's inroads in Nepal and Bhutan, as well as to counter revisions in its Kashmir policy, India had been exhibiting more interest in the Tibetan affairs. While India considers Tibet as a part of China, events related to the radicalization of the Tibetans inside and outside due to no progress in the then China-Tibet talks, have potential consequences to the security and stability in the border regions of India. India also has to gear up to a post-Dalai Lama situation. A post-Dalai Lama situation could provide opportunities and challenges for India to enhance border trade and the overall bilateral relations, since China had configured Tibet as one of its main core interests and had stiffened its position on the Tibetan émigré issue over the last three decades.[17]

Fourthly, while India tested nuclear devices partly after accusing Beijing of furthering nuclear and ballistic missile transfers to Pakistan in the 1990s,[18] the "no first use" doctrine of India and China did provide for cushions between the two, although China and the US have been critical of the India's nuclear tests and the subsequent sanctions and 1172 resolution by the United Nations

Security Council.[19] Today, China continues to follow a balance of power policy between New Delhi and Islamabad by insisting that India sign the international arms control and disarmament measures. The nuclear factor divided both India and China with the former approaching US, Russia, France and other countries for technology and commerce cooperation in the civilian sphere. When India had signed the civil nuclear deal with the US in 2006, China was either critical of the deal and the proposal for a "clean waiver" at the IAEA and NSG in 2008 or had offered to "Grandfather" Pakistan's nuclear plants at Chashma. As a result of these differences and for security reasons, India had been testing and acquiring newer and more potent ballistic missiles like Agni III, IV and V and interceptor missiles[20] . India is also strengthening its conventional deterrence by strengthening its land and air forces after China's land air force preparations in Tibet and elsewhere posed concerns for India.[21] Indian defence establishment had made several statements in this regard. For instance, the then Indian Army chief Gen. Deepak Kapoor said on October 7, 2009, that the army is preparing for two theatre wars with Pakistan and China under nuclear conditions.[22] Indian defence minister A K Anthony told at the first Consultative Committee meeting of new Members of Parliament attached to the Defence Ministry on November 16, 2009, that India should "build asymmetric capabilities against superior forces" and called for enhancing strategic reach of the air force.[23]

Fifthly, China had argued that it is now dependent on the Indian Ocean Region heavily for its oil imports which crossed above 280 million tonnes in 2011—with 80 percent of these passing through the Malacca Straits.[24] To offset any energy flow disruptions, the Chinese navy is now preparing for what has been termed as "string of pearls" in the region of setting up dual-use facilities. For Pehrson, China's efforts at "string of pearls" poses challenges to the US control in the region, although the Indian navy had also expressed concerns of the growing China's naval activities.[25] China had dispatched 11 naval contingents to the region ostensibly to counter piracy threats to its commerce. However, some of these contingents also include amphibious ships, indicating to missions other than countering non-state actors. To counter these, India had been mobilizing its naval forces in the region in conjunction with the other navies of the region and, in its 2007 maritime doctrine, had configured the region as of primary interest and the Gulf of Aden and South China Sea of secondary importance.[26] As a result the Indian navy is not only engaging itself in the west but also in the east—with Japan, South Korea and

Southeast Asian navies, specifically Vietnam. Also, India's Oil and Natural Gas Commission's Videsh Limited had signed deals with Vietnam to drill for energy resources in South China Sea, although it withdrew from No. 127 oil block, while re-emerging in No. 128 block.

Sixthly, India is learning from China's experience of benefiting from the US even as it had retained its strategic autonomy. For instance, China-US relations had been stable despite contentious issues between both, such as on Taiwan, Tibet, South China Sea, Japan, South Korea, human rights, currency devaluation, trade surpluses, violation of intellectual property rights, etc. As mentioned above, since 2005, the US had also changed its policies vis-à-vis India and today both India and the US are able to expand bilateral relations "based on defence ties" as US Department of Defence Deputy Secretary Ashton Carter said in mid-2012. India was able to procure sophisticated defence equipment from the US to the tune of nearly $10 billion with an overall figure reaching possibly $20 billion. Besides, nearly 50 structured meetings took place between the two in 2011 with wide-ranging dialogues on issues related to counter-terrorism, maritime issues, regional stability, etc. Both have also expanded the dialogue process to include Japan and three such trilateral meeting took place till 2012.

Multilateral Initiatives

Apart from its own initiatives in addressing challenges and opportunities posed by China, India has also undertaken multilateral cooperative measures with a number of countries. India has entered into such ties with Beijing with the assumption that such ties will be able to bind bilateral relations as with the fulfillment of mutual interests, specifically in the World Trade Organization, Doha Rounds, climate change proposals and the like. Nevertheless, it appears to New Delhi that cooperation with China in the multilateral sphere has not been able to improve bilateral relations, specifically on the contentious issues such as the territorial disputes as enlisted above.

India-Russia-China trilateral meetings, sometimes mentioned as "strategic triangle" among the three countries, originated in the in the proposal of the then Russian Prime Minister Primakov during his visit to New Delhi in December 1998 where he expressed interest in forming a "strategic triangle" with India and China in the wake of the US air strikes on Iraq in the Operation Desert Fox. He stated: "A lot depends in the region on the policies of China, Russia and India. If we succeed in establishing a strategic triangle, it will be very good." Since then the three held, at the governmental level, 11 meetings of the foreign ministers of the three countries till April 2012. Trilateral cooperation is reflected in joint coordination at the United Nations discussions on Myanmar, Iran, Libya, Syria and other hot spots, counter-terrorism, sensitivity on sovereignty related issues, promoting trade and investments, etc. The trilateral also called for the reorganisation of the UN Security Council, including Indian candidature, although, in implicit terms. Nevertheless, the trilateral had not been able to achieve concrete progress in enhancing cooperation among the three.

The above trilateral countries also, nevertheless, had expanded into another larger grouping, the BRICS, with Brazil and South Africa joining the multilateral process. This grouping had met four times since 1999 till 2012, with the fifth meeting poised to be held in South Africa in March 2013. The specific focus of this grouping is to voice the perspectives of the developing countries in terms of the ill-effects of financial crisis and trade protectionism of the western countries. India's interests in the above multilateral institutions is to protect its sovereignty and economic and social development interests in the light of a series of new developments like unilateralism, globalization, climate change proposals, etc.

India had also joined another set of multilateral institutions such as Shanghai Cooperation Organization (as an observer). In April 2004, India had applied for membership in the SCO, but had not been granted so far due to lack of consensus in the SCO but more possibly due to the Chinese opposition.[27] Indian interests in this grouping primarily are to counter terrorism and secure energy resources.

Another grouping where India had become more active, despite the initial opposition of China to New Delhi's membership is the East Asian Summit. India's policy of economic engagement with the Southeast and East region, according to Zhao Gancheng, is legitimate in attracting investments and technology and that these are broadly in the interests of China itself.[28] However, other Chinese think that India's policy of engagement with this region, although appears legitimate, may be detrimental to China in the sense that Indian naval entry into South China Sea and the Pacific, apart from the positioning of Andaman & Nicobar joint command in the vicinity of the vulnerable Straits of Malacca's, is intended to balance China. A more pronounced and hawkish view in China is that Indian role in Southeast Asia, although unveiled a step-by-step approach, is aimed at countering China by first evolving closer relations with Vietnam, Japan and Singapore and then with the United States. This third position views Indian role as part of the strategic containment of the region, which is traditionally considered by China as its sphere of influence and that this should be opposed by China by adopting a multi-pronged approach.

Besides these initiatives at the multilateral level, India is also engaged in dialogue processes and bilateral cooperative frameworks. Indian role in the multilateral discussions at the Shangri-la dialogue process at Singapore, Indian naval exercises with Vietnam, Japan and other Southeast Asian countries have all been stepped up. India's swift naval assistance during the Tsunami tragedy in the region in 2004-05 was welcomed by the concerned.

Conclusion

The above discussion indicates that the Indian responses towards China's rise have been comprehensive, measured, forthcoming and keeping in view the overall strategic situation. While protecting its core interests on the sovereignty and territorial integrity issues, India has been expanding ties with China in mutually beneficial areas such as trade, investments, multilateral coordination at the UN, on climate change proposals and the like. Although India realizes that such multilateral cooperation with China has not led to any perceptive progress in resolving outstanding disputes with China, New Delhi feels that it is important to remain engaged with China on the mutually beneficial development related issues. Yet, there is a thought process in India that China's rise is comprehensive and strategic in its orientation with issues related to international and regional power configurations. Any change in the current configurations of power—which is happening gradually with the rise of China—would prove to be detrimental to the India's long-term interests. While the ability of China to displace the dominant power of the United States is still remote and is subjected to contention between China and the US, such a contingency still needs to be addressed by New Delhi, specifically as asymmetries of power is widening enormously between India and China. Although, the Indian idea of "Enough space in Asia" is still a short to medium term contingency, it could serve to postpone conflict with Beijing and increase areas of mutually beneficial cooperation and breathing time to enhance India's comprehensive national power.

NOTES AND REFERENCES

1. For instance, Prime Minister Manmohan Singh stated in the parliament: "...China is our strategic partner. We have a multi-faceted relationship with China....There is enough space—I have said so often—for both China and India to develop and contribute to global peace, stability and prosperity. We do not see our relations with China in antagonistic terms. We have a large trading relationship, we consult each other on global issues, whether in the G-20 process on climate change or terrorism, and we share a common commitment to maintain peace and tranquillity on our border." See "PM's reply to the debate in the Lok Sabha on the President's address" June 9, 2009, accessed at http://pmindia.gov.in/pmsinparliament.php?nodeid=36, accessed on June 14, 2013
2. Liu Qingcai. "Xin shiqi Zhongguo de mulin waijiao zhengsi" [Good neighbourliness foreign policy of China in the new period] Guoji Guancha [International Survey], May 2005.
3. Under these conditions, a writer argued that China's policy towards the region ought to be that of "huxin, huli, pingdeng, banzuo" [mutual trust, mutual benefit, equality and cooperation]. See Fu Yong, "21 shiji chu zhong nanya anquan huanqing yu Zhongguo" [Early 21st century Central South Asian security environment and China's western areas security] Shijie Jingji Yanjiu (Studies of World Economy) 12 (2003).
4. Cheng Ruisheng, "Lun ZhongYin Zhanlue hezuo huoban guanxi" [On Sino-Indian Strategic Partnership] Guoji Wenti Yanjiu [International Studies Research] 1 (2007), pp. 13-18. Cheng argued that despite some setbacks, India-China relations are to disprove pessimists about their growing relations as the political foundation between the two is still strong.
5. Shi Xuewei, "Zhongguo nanya zhanlue zhong de keshemier wenti" [Kashmir Issue in China's South Asia Strategy] Luoyang Shifan Xueyuan Xuebao [Journal of Luoyang Normal University] July 2011, pp. 49-54
6. In the wake of both India and Pakistan acquiring nuclear capabilities, such an issue would be crucial for the stability of the region as a whole. See Zhang Li, "Zhongguo de Nanya waijiao yu Keshimier wenti" [China's diplomacy towards South Asia and Kashmir issue] Nanya Yanjiu Qikan [South Asia Quarterly] 1(2006). Some Chinese have argued that the realistic solution to the Kashmir issue is to recognise the line of control between India and Pakistan. See Wang Changming, "YinBa zai Keshemier wenti shangde kunjing yu chulu" [The predicament and solution to the Kashmir issue between India and Pakistan] Zhida Xuebao [Workers College Journal] April 2008, pp. 43-46 and 70
7. Wen Fude, "Nanya zai Zhongguo xibu da kaifa zhanlue zhong de diwei he zuoyong" [South Asia's Position and Function for the Western Development Strategy of China] Dangdai Yadai [Contemporary Asia-Pacific] 3(2002).
8. Wang Weiluo, "Water Resources and the Sino-Indian Strategic Partnership" China Rights Forum No. 1, 2006 originally published at China Information Center, accessed at http://www.observechina.net/info/artshow.asp?ID=37736&ad=1/10/2006
9. Lin Liangguang, Ye Zhengjia and Han Hua, Eds. Dangdai Zhongguo yu Nanya guojia guanxi [Contemporary China and South Asian countries relations] (Beijing, Social Sciences Reference Publications, 2001).
10. John W. Garver, *Protracted Contest: Sino-Indian Rivalry in the Twentieth Century,* Oxford University Press, New Delhi, 2001; Mohan Malik, "The China factor in the India-Pakistan Conflict" Occasional Paper Series Asia-Pacific Center for Security Studies, Honolulu, November 2002; Shao Zhiyong, "India's big power dream" Beijing Review, April 12, 2001 p. 10
11. Ai Yang, "China may finance Pakistan reactors", China Daily June 23, 2010 accessed at

http://www.chinadaily.com.cn/world/2010-06/23/content_10005608.htm, accessed on June 14, 2013

12. Shen Dingli, "Don't shun the idea of setting up overseas military bases" January 28, 2010 accessed at http://www.china.org.cn/opinion/2010-01/28/content_19324522.htm, accessed on June 14, 2013. Also see, Saibal Dasgupta, "China mulls setting up military base in Pakistan," *The Times of India*, January 28, 2010 accessed at http://articles.timesofindia.indiatimes.com/2010-01-28/china/28120878_1_karokoram-highway-military-bases-north-west-frontier-province, accessed on June 14, 2013

13. "China and Nepal" available on April 12, 2007 at http://www.fmprc.gov.cn/eng/4402.html and China Ministry of Foreign Affairs Policy Planning Division, Zhongguo Waijiao 2011 [China's Diplomacy 2012] (Beijing: Ministry of Foreign Affairs, 2012).

14. Kanwal Sibal, "India's Foreign Policy: Future Options" Third Y B Chavan Memorial Lecture, Institute of Defence Studies & Analyses, New Delhi, November 30, 2012 accessed at http://idsa.in/YBChavanMemorialLecture.

15. See for a comprehensive work in this regard, John W Garver, "Development of China's Overland Transportation Links with Central, South-West and South Asia," *The China Quarterly*, No. 185, March, 2006, pp. 1-22

16. "PM's address at the India-China Economic, Trade and Investment Summit" January 14, 2008 accessed at http://pmindia.gov.in/speech-details.php?nodeid=621, accessed on June 14, 2013 and "Transcript of PM's onboard press conference enroute Astana to New Delhi" April 16, 2011 accessed at http://pmindia.gov.in/press-details.php?nodeid=1226, accessed on June 14, 2013

17. See Leon Bai, "Resolving the India-China Boundary Dispute: Incentivising Cooperation, Enlarging Bargaining Space and Promoting Constructive Strategies" Observer Research Foundation Occasional Paper #33, May 2012.

18. As Indian Prime Minister Vajpayee said in a letter to the then US President Clinton that the "deteriorating security environment" in the neighbourhood drove India to test nuclear weapons. Further, we have an overt nuclear weapon state on our borders, a state which committed armed aggression against India in 1962. Although our relations with that country have improved in the last decade or so, an atmosphere of distrust persists mainly due to the unresolved border problem. To add to the distrust that country has materially helped another neighbour of ours to become a covert nuclear weapons state.

    See Indian Prime Minister's Letter to the US President, May 13, 1998 accessed at http://pmindia.nic.in/

19. Zhang Jiegen, "Contemporary Indian Strategic Culture and its Nuclear Strategy" International Review Spring 2007, Volume 46 pp. 84-98

20. In 1983, Indian Defence Research and Development Organisation launched an integrated guided missile development programme and developed several tactical and strategic missiles. Of these, mention should be made of—as a part of its "credible" deterrence capability—the launch of Agni II in April 1999 which has a combat radius of about 2,000 km and payload of one tonne. In April 2007, India successfully tested Agni III IRBM with an estimated combat radius of more than 3,000 km and payload carrying capacity of 1.5 tonnes, while an earlier test in July 2006 proved to be a failure. In April 2012, India launched a 5,000 km range Agni V.

21. Ramesh V. Phadke, "People's Liberation Army Air Force (PLAAF): Shifting Airpower Balance and Challenges to India's Security" Center for International Security and Cooperation Stanford University Working Paper, February 2002.

22. "Indian Army can counter Chinese threat: Army Chief" October 7, 2009, accessed at

http://news.oneindia.in/2009/10/07/indian-army-can-counter-chinese-threat-army-chief.-html

23. "India should build asymmetric warfare capabilities: Anthony," *The Indian Express*, November 16, 2009.
24. A Chinese report estimated that about ten percent of global trade volume passes through the Indian Ocean Region, of which a significant portion belongs to that of petroleum trade. See "Yinduyang" [Indian Ocean], 2007 accessed at http://www.21page.net/world_geography/indian_ocean.asp, accessed on July 16
25. Christopher J. Pehrson, "String of Pearls: Meeting the challenge of China's Rising Power across the Asian littoral" Strategic Studies Institute, US Army War College, July, 2006. On a Chinese perspective of the subject see Geng Yinzeng, Zhongguo ren yu Yinduyang [Chinese People and Indian Ocean] (Zhengzhou, 1997)
26. Integrated Headquarters Ministry of Defence (Navy), *Freedom to Use the Seas: India's Maritime Military Strategy*, New Delhi, 2007, p. 61
27. "India pitches for full membership of SCO" October 27, 2005, accessed at http://www.siliconindia.com/shownews/India_pitches_for_full_membership_of_SCO-nid-29799.html, accessed on June 30, 2009; also see Indian foreign ministry spokesman's statement, "India supports basic SCO principles: official" Xinhua June 13, 2006 accessed at http://english.scosummit2006.org/en_zxbb/2006-06/13/content_551.htm, accessed on June 30, 2009
28. Zhao Gancheng, "India: Look East Policy and Role in Asian Security Architecture" Position Paper at the SIIS-Brookings Conference on Regionalism in Asia, Shanghai, December 11-12, 2006 accessed at http://www.siis.org.cn/forumenglish/brookings/gancheng4.pdf; This is also available at *Indian Ocean Digest* 42 (21) July-December 2006

Chapter 4

Dynamics of India-China Relations in a Changing Global Geo-Political Environment

Gurudas Das

The trajectory of India's China Policy has transformed from (i) bilateral brotherhood (1949-61) to (ii) bilateral hostility and disengagement (1962-87) to (iii) limited political engagement (1988-2000) and then to (iv) growing economic engagement (2001 onwards) in post-cold war era. While the Sino-Indian relationships during the first phase of bilateral brotherhood (1949-62) was guided by the principle of *Panchsheel* which includes (i) Mutual respect for each other's territorial integrity and sovereignty, (ii) Mutual non-aggression, (iii) Mutual non-interference in each other's internal affairs, (iv) Equality and mutual benefit, and (v) Peaceful co-existence, the second phase of bilateral hostility and disengagement (1962-87) was guided by nationalistic security perception mediated by strategic cold-war alliances, the third phase of limited political engagement (1988-2000) was guided by realistic national security perception, and the fourth phase of growing economic engagement (2001 onwards) was guided by economic pragmatism as both the countries have eventually realized that economic growth is the primary source of national security rather than military capabilities.

The Sino-Indian relations have, thus, followed an oscillatory path of convergence-divergence-convergence. The initial convergence of interests followed from the facts that both India and China were born in an international environment of bipolarity characterized by the cold-war hostility between the two superpowers (USA and USSR). The national interests of both the countries necessitated that they keep a position of equi-distance from both the superpowers so that they were not drawn into the cold-war hostility while working for their respective national development. Both the countries found the Non-Aligned Movement as a suitable platform for furtherance of their national interests and hence joined hands in order to strengthen the Movement as an alternative to global bipolarity.

However, the consolidation of state power in both the countries—Chinese Southern Thrust towards Tibet and India's Forward Policy towards the McMahon Line—had brought them to face off each other. The Tibetan Factor—which marked Chinese occupation of Tibet and consequent migration of a huge Tibetan population into India including the Dalai Lama and their accommodation by India—acted as the fissure in Sino-Indian relations.[1] Instead of realizing the fact that being the land of the Buddha, India cannot deny a shelter to the Tibetans although India does not harbor any territorial claim over Tibet, China viewed India's humanistic position in relation to the displaced Tibetans as an act of deliberate hostility. The result was China's unprovoked war against India which had abruptly ended the India-China honeymoon in 1962. Thereafter, both the countries were drawn into the orbit of cold-war stratagem. While the Sino-Soviet split (1960-89) drifted China towards USA as China wanted to balance one superpower with another as part of her national security strategy, India-China war (1962) drifted India towards USSR as India wanted to play off the Chinese threat as well as break the cordoned off situation by the cold-war axis consisting of China, USA and Pakistan. Thus, national interests complemented with strategic cold war alliance took India and China to a divergent path.[2]

With the collapse of USSR in 1989 and its subsequent breakdown in 1991, states in the international system are relieved of the cold-war crafted security architecture and plunged into forging new strategic partnership even with the one-time rivals. Both India and China broke a quarter century long breach in their relationships since 1962 and courted each other *albeit* with cautious steps following the visit of Indian Prime Minister Rajiv Gandhi to Beijing in 1988. With the process of globalization making headway in both the countries resulting into spectacular economic success for them, economic pragmatism took the centre stage in Indian-China relations since the beginning of the 21st century. The second convergence of interests arose from the new realization that it is perhaps the economic strength rather than the military capability that makes a nation secure. Both India and China require a peaceful environment for their growth to take root and to amplify. Of course, it does not altogether deny the role of military strength in enhancing the status of a nation in the global power game. However, both the countries underplay the militaristic threat perceptions in forging bilateral relations and focus on the economic pragmatism in crafting strategic partnership with nations.

This chapter intends to focus on the options that India can weigh while articulating her China policy in a fast changing global geo-political environment characterized by decline of USA as a global economic power, weakening of EU, rise of China, growing Sino-Russian alliance, shift in USA's engagement from Middle East to Asia-Pacific region, decline of Japan and rise of ASEAN.

China's India Policy: The Interplay of Geo-Politics and Geo-Economics

Understanding China has not only been a great challenge to India alone but also for the world at large primarily due to regimented and controlled nature of intellectual exercises. Unlike the rest of the world, Chinese thought process is filtered through ideological power centre and hence free-wheeling of individual ideas is not allowed in China. As a result, fuller understanding of Chinese mind suffers from inadequacy. Nonetheless, an attempt is made in this section to construct China's India policy based on fragmented information, behavioural attitude of China towards India and analyses made by the strategic analysts on India-China relations.

The underlying hypothesis behind China's India policy has metamorphosed from an equal partner (1949-62) to an irritant weak neighbor (1963-2000) and then to an emerging Asian power (2001 onwards). Although, on the establishment of People's Republic of China (PRC) in 1949, the Chinese political leadership under chairman Mao and Premier Zhou Enlai found commonalities with India in terms of challenges that both the nations faced in a bipolar world towards their respective national development cutting across the ideological divide, and hence worked in tandem in the NAM platform, Chinese leadership primarily viewed India as a stooge of imperial power due to India's claim on imperial territorial boundary and status. The harping on the idea of centrality of independent India in Asia, a status she used to enjoy in British India, emergence of Nehru as the spokesperson of the NAM, India's adoption of Forward Policy in the Himalayas to catch up the McMahon Line, following the Chinese southern thrust towards Tibet, which has not been ratified by China, and providing the asylum to the Dalai Lama and Tibetan refugees following Chinese occupation of Tibet in 1959—all these have changed China's India policy during the early 1960s from friendship to hostility. Chairman Mao, one of the foremost political and military strategists, waged a war against India in 1962 and has (i) established the centrality of China in Asia, (ii) succeeded to keep the boundary dispute in the eastern sector alive, and (ii) assumed the leadership of the newly independent countries of the third world.

From 1963 to the end of the cold war, China followed a policy of encirclement of India by forming an axis with Pakistan and USA as India drifted to Soviet Union to hedge from any future security threats from China. China's India policy had also factored into Indo-Soviet relations. However, China did not allow its foreign policy to be Indo-centric and instead made Pakistan to act as a proxy on her behalf in order to contain India within South Asia. Meanwhile, China used the contradictions of bipolar global geopolitical environment in order to enlarge the strategic space and integrate herself with the global system of governance and global production chain. Leveraging from the process of globalization, China has experienced an unprecedented economic growth and transformed herself into a hub of global manufacturing production during the 1980s and 1990s while the two superpowers were engaged in cold war rivalry. Keeping aside ideological differences, China engaged with USA and developed a strong trade relationship which boosted Chinese export to USA market in an unprecedented scale. China opened up herself for Western investment and technology and used her reserve army of labour force in perfect tandem to create the growth miracle within three decades. Thus, while India was trapped in regional conflict with Pakistan, China leapfrogged herself to global power. China looked at India as weak and irritating neighbor which is no match to her.

While in spite of change in global geo-political environment following the collapse of Soviet Union in 1991, China quietly continued to hold on the growth momentum as the USA was bogged down with the Middle East, India also started opening up and embraced economic reforms resulting into faster economic growth and within a short span of time transformed herself as the hub of global service industry, pharmaceutical industry, research and development services, space research, biotechnology and telecommunication services. This new found economic growth has also enabled India to modernize her military forces and expand her strategic space among different nations. India's nuclear test in 1998 and growing Indo-US cooperation have suddenly changed the image of India among the comity of nations in general and in the eyes of the Chinese leadership in particular. Today, China no more views India as a "weak and irritating neighbor" rather recognizes India as an emerging Asian power.

Contemporary China's India Policy is, to a large extent, informed of both the future projections about India's role vis-à-vis China and present policy imperatives to secure future interest of the Chinese nation. While the former is largely shaped by the orthodox militaristic and strategic analysts, the latter is shaped by the reformist think tanks.

China's India Policy: The Orthodox View

1. The orthodox view, as articulated by Zhang Wenmu of the China Institutes of Contemporary International Relations (CICIR) asserts that India cherishes an intention to separate Tibet from China. Tibetan independence will enable India to create a buffer zone between China and India. This will enable India to take bolder action on the South Asian continent and subsequently, in the Indian Ocean region, without the fear of being attacked from front and rear. Besides India, Western world's future geopolitical strategy is also to split China's western part to create a political barrier like Tibet or Xinjiang between China and the oil-producing countries in Central Asia. This will enable the West to control permanently the world's geographic and energy center. This dovetailing of political interests of India to that of resource interest of the West might lead to the formation of an anti-Chinese coalition which will then pose a tremendous challenge to the security and integrity of the Chinese nation.[3]
2. The orthodox view assesses the future role of India vis-à-vis China as future rival. Chinese Academy of Military Science's (AMS) assessment of India show that China is:
   - Inferior to India in naval power
   - Stronger than India in long-range missiles
   - Inferior to India in overall weapons technology

- Lower than India in defense spending per capita
- Higher than India in overall defense
- Superior, but "the superiority is not great[4]

3. Chinese orthodox view is concerned about India's significant achievement in military affairs during the past few decades. It has been observed that India's capability in developing the science and technology and their use for the production of defense goods has largely helped in catapulting its military power. Now India has the capacity to build large vessels and submarines. It designs and produces aircraft carriers, nuclear submarines, missile destroyers, and equips Russian-made C-grade nuclear submarines with medium-range missiles. The new tanks produced by India can resist high-speed armor piercing shells and anti-tank bombs, and are of world standard. India has started to manufacture modern light fighters. The light fighters have modern navigation and aiming systems, and can have the capacity of continuous flight and inflight fueling. Such fighters are equivalent to M-27s. India will soon enter the ranks of the top-level world military powers.[5]
4. Indian naval power is a great concern for China. India's Navy now ranks 7th in the world and it is one of a small number of countries in the world, and the only one in South Asia, to possess aircraft carriers. Chinese orthodox school apprehends that with new-found economic success, India's naval power will further rise in the 21st century. Indian naval fleet is capable of extending its naval defense line 600 nautical miles beyond a blue-water fleet with a nuclear combat capability. Indian Navy's control of the Indian Ocean, particularly of the two strategic channels of the Persian Gulf and the Strait of Malacca, in the event of maritime cooperation between India and USA is likely to pose security threats to sea lanes vital for China's energy security as the lion's share of crude oil that China imports come from the Middle East countries.

   In order to secure the oil supply routes, China appears to have adopted a two-pronged strategy. First, China is consistently making efforts to increase its influence in the Indian Ocean through the "string of pearl" strategy which involves construction of ports at Gwadar in Pakistan, Hambantota in Sri Lanka, modernization of Chittagong port in Bangladesh and construction of port at Coco Island in Myanmar.

Second, China is working for the establishment of transit corridors from Gwadar port to Xinjiang through Pakistan and Karakoram Highway, from Chittagong port to Yunan through Myanmar, and from Coco Island to Yunan via Myanmar in order to move oil in the event sea lanes are choked off.

5. There is a growing realization in China that India will emerge as an Asia Pacific power in the 21st century as it possesses great potential for development so far as population and territorial size and regional influence are concerned. It is in the Chinese interest to take note of this fact and adjust accordingly.[6] However, the rise of India is not free of challenges. There are a host of "restricting factors" like weak governance, challenges of poverty, divisive religious and caste factors and rising ultranationalist forces gaining ground in the political power structure which will act as the stumbling block towards speedy national growth.
6. Does India's economic development matter to China? Chinese analysts feel that although India is emerging as China's main competitor in international funds, technology and commodity markets, theirs is "not a life or death relationship," because China's economy is stronger. The growth momentum in China will outpace the same in India and hence, in the near future, India cannot become "China's replacement market".[7]
7. The Chinese orthodox school is also critical about India's growing defense ties with Mongolia, South Korea, Vietnam, Indonesia, and other countries in South East Asia which China feels its exclusive domain.[8]
8. India's growing role in ASEAN, enhancement of its relation with Japan and Australia also concern the Chinese strategic analysts. They are worried about either India or Japan becoming part of a future balance of power system in Asia that may emerge in response to a common perceived threat from China.[9]
9. However, the Chinese analysts are confident that neither India nor Japan can alone pose any serious threat to China. In the decades ahead, an Asian multinational security coalition to deter China would have to include several larger powers, roughly equivalent to Chinese economic and military capacity. Using the Comprehensive National Power (CNP) scores of Chinese analysts, for example, it could be

calculated that Japan, Russia, and India would be needed to balance China.[10]

China's India Policy: The Reformist View

1. The reformist view advocates the fact that both China and India need to come out of colonial legacy as far as the border dispute between them is concerned. These two Asian neighbours cannot go on fighting for ever and a negotiated settlement has to be sorted out keeping each other's interest in mind. Both the nations need to address each other's sensitivities and war should not be considered any option for the future settlement of contested issues. Long civilization and historical associations need to be brought into focus while crafting the bilateral relations instead of conflicts between them in the recent past.
2. With the gradual unfolding of a multipolar world structure, both India and China will have sufficient space to grow and scope to contribute in redesigning the global geo-political architecture.
3. China apprehends that as the current hegemon, USA will circumvent her transition to global power and hence it is important for China to engage India so that South Asian landmass is incorporated in the Chinese strategic space.
4. On the way to ascendancy, China needs a stable backyard and hence resolution of India-Pakistan problem is of Chinese interest.
5. Given the longstanding India-Russia relationship, the Primakov Triangle, a coalition among China, Russia and India, might be useful for countering USA's global hegemony and establishing multipolar world structure where China will play a decisive role in global affairs.
6. If 21st century is to be Asian century, China and India need to accommodate each other.

India's China Policy: The Interplay of Geo-Politics and Geo-Economics

India's China policy has metamorphosed from an equal partner (1949-62) to a hostile but rising neighbor (1963-91) and then to an emerging global power (1992 onwards).

On independence, India's foreign policy, under the stewardship of Jawaharlal Nehru, aimed at creating a niche for the newly independent countries in a bipolar global geo-political environment keeping equidistance from both the superpowers in order to accelerate the national economic growth. India found a natural ally in China as both the countries were facing the similar challenges in advancing their national development agenda. Nehru was an idealist and he felt that commonality of interests vis-à-vis the challenges to national development would bind India and China in such an extricable way that bilateral issues between them could be resolved amicably. While India adopted Forward Policy in the Himalayas to catch up the McMohan Line in response to Chinese southern thrust, Nehru expected China to acknowledge India's interest in the Himalayas the way India did it in case of Tibet. Nehru's expectation was shattered while China waged a war on India in 1962 and felt betrayed.

From 1963 to the collapse of Soviet Union in 1991, India maintained a studied silence about China, tilted towards Soviet Union as a strategy to improve national security environment, focused on the capacity building in terms of defense, technology, and economy, insulated herself from global geo-political theatre, directed her energy to counter Pakistan and restricted her ambition within South Asia. However, India was closely watching the development taking place in China particularly in the field of the Chinese economy which made Indian policy makers restive and instilled an urgency to break away from the state-led economic growth model characterized by low growth syndrome. Indian policy makers quietly learned from China and replicated Chinese model of growth through the creation of growth enclaves and strategy of export-led growth. As China outpaced India all most in all fronts, India realized that its strategy of disengagement vis-à-vis China would not work anymore and if India is to settle the bilateral border disputes, it could not be achieved without bilateral engagement. It was this realization that prompted India to re-engage China since 1988 following the visit of Prime Minister Rajiv Gandhi to Beijing.

With the collapse of Soviet Union in 1991, although India lost the security blanket that USSR used to provide in a bipolar global geo-political environment, India became free from the predicaments of bipolarity and charted out its own strategic space through the development of strategic partnerships with other countries. Initiation of economic reforms since 1991, adoption of Look East Policy, replacement of state-led growth model by market-led growth model, and graduation of integration of the economy with the global market—all these enabled India to break the shackles of low growth and charted the path for high growth within a short span of two decades. Sustained economic growth has allowed India the confidence to "de-hyphenate" itself from Pakistan, and pursue broader and more ambitious foreign policy goals.

Although the collapse of Soviet Union has graduated China to a global power, India feels that the 1998 nuclear test and post-cold war emerging strategic alliance with USA and other regional powers and organizations have largely helped her to reduce the power gap with China. Even though India lags substantially behind China particularly in terms of economic growth and military strength, the contemporary India is better positioned in protecting her territorial integrity and national security compared to India of 1962.

Like China's India policy, contemporary India's China Policy is also informed of both the future projections about China's role vis-à-vis India and present policy imperatives to secure future national interest of India. While the former is largely shaped by the orthodox militaristic and strategic analysts, the latter is shaped by the reformists' perception of national interests.

India's China Policy: The Orthodox View

1. The orthodox school is concerned about Chinese military buildup in Tibet. China's alleged deployment of nuclear-capable intermediate range ballistic missile, intercontinental missile, increase in Border Defense Regiments and construction of airfields to support the operation of fighter aircrafts and to enhance airlifting capacity of the Chinese army—all these are causes of concern that require matching response from India to deter any future border conflict.[11] As a minimum deterrence to the threat to territorial integrity, India has also decided to deploy the Brahmos—the supersonic cruise missile—and increase the troop strength in the Eastern Sector in coming years.
2. Indian orthodox school finds a pattern in China's repeated claim over Arunachal Pradesh and deployment of additional defense capabilities across the border in Tibet. In the Chinese official documents, Arunachal Pradesh was not referred as the Southern Tibet before 2005. It has also been noted with great anxiety that China is increasingly orchestrating her political claim over Arunachal Pradesh and military buildup across the border. China has even gone to the extent to lodge protests against the visit of Indian leaders in Arunachal Pradesh and

denying visas to people from this state citing the logic that since Arunachal Pradesh is a part of China, people from this region do not require any visa. In view of all these, in case India does not formulate a strategic response in terms of military preparedness then 1962 history may repeat itself.[12]

3. India's orthodox school is also concerned about China-Pakistan nexus. It is only well known that China has brought Pakistan into her strategic design in South Asia. The age old strategic saying that "enemy's enemy is my friend" well explains Sino-Pakistan alliance against India. Not only China has helped in arming but also in acquiring Pakistan nuclear and missile capability. In response to Indo-US civil nuclear deal, China has agreed to build nuclear reactors for Pakistan. For a long time, while China has leapfrogged to a global power, it succeeded to keep Indian foreign policy Pakistan-centric. The orthodox school is also suspicious of Chinese massive infrastructure building in Pakistan Occupied Kashmir (POK) which India claims as her part.[13]
4. The orthodox school is severely concerned with China's unprecedented military modernization in all lines of defense—land, sea and air. China's increasing defense spending in the absence of credible threats to China's national security transcends the requirements of a "defensive build-up' and the magnitude of China's military build-up in peace time. China's defense spending is the second highest in the world after the USA. China is heavily investing for making stealth fighter jet, aircraft carrier, improved version of submarines, anti-ship ballistic missiles, submarine launched ballistic missiles (SRBM), and acquiring new heights in space and cyber wars.[14]
5. The orthodox school is also concerned about Chinese penetration in Indian Ocean. It views Chinese strategy of "String of Pearl" directed against curbing the domination of Indian Navy in Indian Ocean. Chinese ambition to become a two-ocean nation and their assertion that "Indian Ocean does not mean India's Ocean" clearly manifests China's strategy to become a sea power.[15]
6. Indian orthodox school worries about Chinese strategy of encirclement of India. China has stepped up its economic, political and military engagement with countries in South Asia and South

East Asia like Pakistan, Myanmar, Nepal, Bangladesh and Sri Lanka which India considers to be her strategic space.

7. The orthodox school is concerned about China's Kashmir policy. Earlier China refrained from taking any side on the Kashmir issue but of late it started to issue staple visa to the people of Kashmir clearly indicating that China does not consider Kashmir to be an undisputed part of India. In spite of the fact that India recognizes Tibet as a part of China and India also accepted one-China policy in regards to the Taiwan dispute, China has not reciprocated.[16]
8. It has been observed that no substantial progress has been made for resolving India-China border dispute even after several border talks and Joint Working Groups meetings primarily due to the lack of political will on the part of China. China continues to exploit border disputes as strategic pressure points to gain territorial and strategic advantages. The recent hardening of Chinese policy towards Arunachal Pradesh is seen as a pressure tactic to woo India not to join the USA's Asia-Pacific security strategy designed to contain China.

India's China Policy: The Reformist View

1. The reformist school suggests that, as China has already emerged as the economic superpower and poised to become a military superpower by the middle of the century, India needs to engage China rather than joining the containment bandwagon.
2. India needs to learn from the trajectory of Chinese growth. India needs unfettered peaceful environment to continue the momentum of economic growth. If economic growth is faltered by any reason, then the strategic global geo-economic space is certain to reduce.
3. India needs to work quietly to reduce the economic and security gap vis-à-vis China. India needs to leverage from the complimentarity between the economies of the two countries rather than competing for balance in military power which, it is feared, may derail the economy. Although there is a need for building a minimum deterrence for the protection of national security, India should not join the arm race with China which is primarily directed against USA.
4. India needs to underplay the areas of conflict in bilateral relationship with China and stress upon the areas of cooperation to engage China. Instead of forming an alliance with USA against China, India must

chart out her own geo-political strategy aiming to strengthen the national goals and interests through a well-crafted policy of cooperative security.

Both the orthodox and reformist views provide inputs in crafting the structure of bilateral relationship between nations. As the foreign policy decision making involves complex processes, it is difficult to conjecture as to which of these two views dominate over the other. Certainly, the balance is influenced by a host of factors like contemporary dynamics of global and regional geo-politics, bilateral policy reciprocity, national interests, and futuristic projection of national strengths and weaknesses, etc.

Conclusion

Emergence of China as an economic superpower that is destined to compete with USA for global power has provided a window of opportunities for India to exert greater leadership on the world stage. As the global geo-political environment is heading towards the replication of another cold-war type syndrome between the existing superpower (USA) and the rising superpower (China), although characteristically different from the earlier USA-Soviet Union led cold war paradigm, India can leverage from this and chart out her own path of national development by engaging China economically and USA politically. Integrating economic benefits from China and technological benefits from the West, India can emerge as a global power in the years to come.

Where does India stand in terms of national power? According to Chinese assessment of the Comprehensive National Power (CNP) of the nations published in January 2006 in a Report on International Politics and Security prepared by the Social Sciences Centre, a government sponsored Chinese think tank, India was ranked 10 with a score of 50.43 while China was ranked 6 with a score of 59.10. However, the study ranked USA 1 (90.62), UK 2 (65.04), Russia 3 (63.03), France 4 (62.00) and Germany 5 (61.93).

A similar study on national power measured in terms of Composite Index of National Capability (CINC) developed by J David Singer has ranked India in 2007 as the 3rd most powerful country in the world with CINC score of 0.073444. However, the study ranked China as the most powerful nation having a CINC score of 0.198578 and ranked USA as the second most powerful nation having a CINC score of 0.142149.

Another study on national power projection, measured in terms of National Power Index (NPI) developed by Atlantic Council, a USA strategic think tank, and calculated by the International Futures Computer Model, for 2020, ranked USA as the first, China second and India third. These rankings remain the same till 2030. But by 2040, China replaces USA and occupies the first position, USA comes down to second, and India remains at the third position. However, by 2050, India climbs one notch up to push USA in the third position while China maintains its lead.

How far these power projections will actualize in the future largely depends on how deftly India responds to the challenges and opportunities likely to arise out of emerging bipolar geo-political environment. Once India emerges as a global power, she will have the strength to negotiate her border dispute with China on equal footing. If India can do a China on China in the future, only then China might swallow her claim on Arunachal Pradesh. Until then, voices from the border will only reverberate in the wilderness.

NOTES AND REFERENCES

1. Swamy Subrahmaniam, *India's China Perspective*, Konark Publishers, New Delhi, 2001.
2. Gurudas Das, *Security and Development in India's North East*, Oxford University Press, New Delhi, 2012.
3. Michael Pillsbury, *China Debates the Future Security Environment*, National Defense University Press, Washington DC, 2000.
4. *ibid*
5. *ibid*
6. *ibid*
7. *ibid*
8. Bilveer Singh, Southeast Asia-India Defence Relations in the Changing Regional Security Landscape, IDSA Monograph Series no 4, IDSA, New Delhi, 2011
9. Michael Pillsbury, 2000, *op.cit.*
10. *ibid*
11. Harinder Singh, Establishing India's Military Readiness: Concerns and Strategy, IDSA Monograph Series No 5, IDSA, New Delhi, 2011.
12. Shailender Arya, "Infrastructure Development and Chinese War Waging Capabilities in Tibet", Journal of Defence Studies, Vol5, No 3, 2011. Also, Namarata Goswami, "China's Territorial Claim on Arunachal Pradesh: Crafting an Indian Response", IDSA, Issue Brief, 2010, accessed at www.idsa.in/system/files/IB_Chinasterrorialclaim.pdf, accessed on June 14, 2013.
13. Mandip Singh, Increasing Chinese Footprint in India's North West: What should India do?, IDSA, 2011, accessed at http://idsa.in/idsacomment/IncreasingChineseFootprintin IndiasNorthWest_msingh_211011, accessed on June 14, 2013.
14. Bhaskar Roy, "China's Unimaginative India Policy", Paper No 4793, South Asia Analysis Group, 2011. Also Arun Sahgal, "Chinese Anti Access Strategy: Conceptualising and

Contextualising an Indian Version," *Journal of Defence Studies*, Vol 5, No 3, 2011.

15. Iskander Rehman, 2011, "An Ocean at the Intersection of the Two Emerging Maritime Narratives," IDSA Issue Brief, accessed at http://idsa.in/system/files/IB_AirSeaBattleConcept.pdf, accessed on June 14, 2013. Also Lalit Kumar, 2011, "Contours of a Possible Indian Riposte to Chinese Agrgresiveness", IDSA Policy Brief, accessed at http://idsa.in/policybrief/ContoursofaPossibleIndianRipostetoChinese Aggressiveness_lkumar_170112, accessed on June 14, 2013.
16. Prashant Kumar Singh, 2010, "Revisiting China's Kashmir Policy", IDSA Comment, accessed at http://www.idsa.in/idsacomments/RevisitingChinasKashmirPolicy_pksingh_011110, accessed on June 14, 2013.

Chapter 5

Arunachal Pradesh in the Sino-Indian Boundary Dispute: Constant Claims, Changing Politics

Jabin T. Jacob

The main point of contention in the Sino-Indian boundary dispute was originally the Aksai Chin area in the Indian northwest. In the mid-1980s, however, the core of the dispute shifted eastward to the Indian state of Arunachal Pradesh. This essay makes the argument that while Arunachal Pradesh remains central to the boundary dispute its significance for the two parties to the dispute has varied over time. For China, the shift in emphasis to Arunachal was in large measure tied to the Tibet question, and this emphasis has, if anything, become more important in recent years as instability and protests in Tibet have increased. For India too, Arunachal's significance has grown, owing mostly due to the increased Chinese attention. But India also appears to be moving from defending Arunachal militarily within a purely bilateral context to defending Arunachal and strengthening Indian claims in the international context.

This essay also argues that Arunachal ought to be seen in the Sino-Indian relationship not only within the context of the boundary dispute but also within the framework of centre-periphery relations in China and India and in the larger context of the differences between the Chinese and Indian political systems. The nature of Arunachal Pradesh's relations with the rest of India, including the Indian central government, is important not just for the

Indian body politic but also for Sino-Indian relations and for Beijing's relations with Tibet. If in India, this centre-periphery relationship is a just and equitable one, maintaining a fair and necessary balance between local aspirations for peaceful and sustainable development alongside national security considerations, then India and Arunachal can become the model to follow for China and Tibet—it is in this way that Arunachal will best fulfill its role as the 'first line of defence for India'.

This essay is divided into four sections including a conclusion. The first section looks at how Arunachal Pradesh is currently involved in the Sino-Indian boundary dispute, the second, looks at how China's stress on Arunachal is a part of its inability to stabilize Tibet; and the third section looks at India's own relationship with Arunachal.

Arunachal and the Boundary Dispute Today

For the Chinese, Arunachal Pradesh may today be at the heart of the Sino-Indian boundary dispute but the boundary dispute itself is increasingly less at the heart of the Sino-Indian relationship. And this appears increasingly the case also for India, even as it does not countenance any territorial concessions or disturbing of settled populations,[1] and remains in general, far more sensitive to the persistence of the boundary dispute than China is.

Indeed, the Special Representative-talks mechanism that China and India began in 2003 and the 2005 Agreement on Political Parameters and Guiding Principles, in essence, signaled that China and India had to resolve their dispute politically rather than purely on the basis of historical or legal factors. This in effect also suggests that resolution of the dispute has now become tied to other factors, such as for example, Chinese perceptions of Indo-U.S. ties, the state of affairs inside Tibet and ups and downs in Sino-Indian economic relations.

If this is so, then the centrality of the boundary dispute itself to Sino-Indian ties must necessarily decrease. On the other hand, incidents of Chinese incursions across the LAC appear to have gone up in recent years (Shukla 2012). And incursions have taken place all along the LAC. Further, even leaving aside the matter of incursions, the Chinese have been particularly vocal on Arunachal Pradesh and Tawang in recent years.[2] The Chinese have reacted sharply to visits to Arunachal by Indian Prime Minister Manmohan Singh in February 2008 (Chaudhury 2008) and October 2009 (*Indian Express*

2009a)), President Pratibha Patil in April 2009 (*Indian Express* 2009c), and Defence Minister AK Antony in February 2012, to mark the 25th anniversary of Arunachal's statehood (Dasgupta 2012). Also in 2009, Beijing objected to the Dalai Lama's visit to Tawang (*Indian Express*, 2009b) and to New Delhi approaching the Asian Development Bank for loans for projects in the Northeast Indian state (Samanta 2009; see also Ministry of External Affairs 2009).

While many of these instances are one-off events, incursions and accusations of the Chinese 'nibbling' away at Arunachali territory have been constant (Author's interviews 2008a, 2011). The other constant problem has been the issuing or denial of Chinese visas to Indian citizens from Arunachal.

Chinese 'Incursions'

The issue of Chinese incursions in Arunachal Pradesh is a long-standing one with reports in the public domain dating back to at least 2003 (*Times of India* 2003). Both the issue of incursions and that of the alleged steady occupation of Indian territory by the Chinese, can be dealt with very simply. As long as there is no agreement between the two sides on the exact alignment of the LAC, neither side can really say that the other is in violation of any agreement or of having intruded into its territory.[3] 'Incursions' by both sides therefore, must be seen as a natural fact of life on the LAC between China and India and will continue, whether out of genuine belief that the territory in question belongs to the side that makes the 'incursion' or out of a need to show presence in areas still infrequently visited by both sides.[4]

Deliberate incursions into areas long-accepted as clearly belonging to the other side's control must be viewed against the background of either local-level belligerence or of the larger context of Sino-Indian relations. While it is certainly possible that local-level army commanders can deliberately engage in provocation, it remains an unlikely scenario given the sensitivity around such actions in both capitals or at least in both militaries. On the other hand, the highest authorities could conceivably sanction deliberate incursions because relations are perceived to be deteriorating on another front or as a form of signaling (such as a warning) or indeed out of a wrong assessment of the possible responses by the other side. For instance, the general increase in Chinese incursions (as seen in Indian media reportage) appears to coincide also with the improvement in Indo-US relations and so can be interpreted as a reflection of Chinese concerns about whether this relationship is aimed at containing China.[5] In this case, it is almost unquestioningly assumed that it is only the Chinese government that can engage in such deliberate provocation and not the Indian government; but, it is not always clear why it is assumed that the Indian government has not engaged or will not engage in such deliberate provocation for the reasons mentioned above.

Meanwhile, it perhaps makes ample military, and often economic, sense to 'nibble' away at territory as it were, or occupy it steadily, if any side thinks it can get away with it and if it has the capability to sustain its presence. Given the still poor state of transport and communication infrastructure on the Indian side and the vastly superior progress made in the same department on the Chinese side, it is but natural that the Chinese will engage in such activity and even have 'succeeded' as far as Indian perceptions are concerned (Author's interviews 2008a, 2011). In any case, the fact remains that China's 'new forward policy'[6] is facilitated by the availability of resources for military modernization and upgradation of infrastructure on its side of the border on the one hand and India's slow speed in getting things moving on the ground (even if resources are no longer such a huge constraint), on the other.

China's Visa Policy for Arunachalis

China's visa policy for Indian citizens from Arunachal Pradesh is another long-standing issue between the two sides.

In the late 1980s, then Arunachal Chief Minister Gegong Apang and Speaker T.L. Rajkumar were denied Chinese visas on the grounds that Arunachalis did not need visas at all since they were 'Chinese citizens' anyway. In 1995, however, a team of four Arunachali women, including the prominent social activist Jarjum Ete, received Chinese visas to participate in the Fourth World Conference on Women in Beijing (Ete 2012). And in 2006, two Arunachali state government ministers Tsering Gyurme and Chawna Mein were also first denied visas before apparently visiting China on tourist visas; the former even visited Tibet (Dholabhai 2007). Similarly, Vishal Nabam, Arunachal Pradesh Congress (I) member, and later an advisor to Arunachal Chief Minister Dorjee Khandu, visited China on a month-long tourist visa the same year (*Economic Times* 2011).

Two cases from 2007 brought the issue to greater prominence at least in India. In April, a team of 48 Indians invited to an international science and technology fair in China, originally included four Arunachalis. However, the invitation was revised later and the Chinese dropped C.P. Namchoom, legislator from Lohit, Tajom Taloh and Tape Bagna, both IAS officers, and Tasso Butung, another official. New Delhi agreed to this arrangement and only 44 eventually went. Next month, however, in a team of over 100 IAS officers on a New Delhi-planned study tour to China, the lone Arunachali officer, Ganesh Koyu, was denied a Chinese visa, again on the grounds that he did not need one (*Financial Express* 2007). This time however, India refused to accept the Chinese action and cancelled the entire delegation's visit in response. It is notable that in between the two trips, Kiren Rijiju, then Member of Parliament from Arunachal Pradesh belonging to the opposition BJP, had raised the issue in Parliament of the April visit that had excluded Arunachalis (Dholabhai 2007). Rijiju himself has travelled to China while a Member of Parliament on a diplomatic passport (Rijiju 2012).

A new development in China's visa policy vis-à-vis Arunchalis was seen in January 2011 when China issued stapled visas to two Arunachalis, copying a policy it had recently adopted with respect to Indian citizens of Jammu and Kashmir. The two Arunachalis—a weightlifter and his coach—had been invited to participate in a weightlifting event by the Chinese Weightlifting Association and were prevented from proceeding by Indian immigration authorities (*Times of India* 2011b; see also Ministry of External Affairs 2011b). In June, five Arunachali members of an Indian karate team to China were also issued stapled visas. The Arunachalis—two officials and three sportspersons, part of a large Indian contingent headed to an Asian-level karate competition—were again stopped at Indian immigration and prevented from proceeding (Kashyap 2012). Interestingly, there were reports earlier, of the Chinese embassy agreeing to issue visas to the Arunachali karatekas after intensive discussions with Indian authorities (*Times of India* 2011a).

In the latest instance, China refused to issue a visa in early January 2012 to an Indian Air Force (IAF) officer, Group Captain M. Panging from Arunachal Pradesh slated to leave for China as part of a 30-member Indian military delegation. The delegation later left with just half the complement of officers that had originally planned to travel. While no information is available so far on the nature of the denial of his visa, it seems unlikely that he was like Apang, considered as not requiring a visa because this would mean that the Chinese were allowing an Indian military officer to enter China freely.

How does one explain this Chinese visa policy? Does this show the

Chinese to be inconsistent or is there a method to be discerned in China's actions? Available information in the public domain does not allow us to reach any definite conclusions. Partly, this is because there are inconsistencies of detail in how the same news event is reported in different English dailies and partly because the reports are not comprehensive enough leaving many crucial questions unanswered or important aspects unaddressed. This reflects either an inability to understand the whole issue in its complexity or a tendency to sensationalize without bothering to get to the root of the matter. The Indian Ministry of External Affairs' statements meanwhile, are often perfunctory and no less opaque.

Broadly, it would appear that China has adopted multiple approaches to issuing visas to Arunachalis. Ordinary civilians, including political leaders from Arunachal Pradesh, it would appear can come under three approaches—no visa required, regular stamped visas or stapled visas. Officials of the central government however, have either been told they did not need visas or, as in the latest case of the IAF officer, refused a visa altogether.[7]

Meanwhile, one could argue that from saying that no visas were required, the issuing of stapled visas to Arunachalis is possibly, a step forward—an acknowledgement that the area in question is disputed, and by implication, amenable to resolution by negotiations. A senior Chinese scholar associated with the Chinese Foreign Ministry-affiliated think-tank, China Institute of International Studies, has argued that stapled visas were only a 'pragmatic' step designed to allow people of Arunachal to visit China, even as his country's position on the dispute remained unchanged (*Economic Times* 2011). Further, refusing visas as in the case of the Arunachali IAF officer, might be considered still another step forward as far as China is concerned given that refusal of visas is a more acceptable practice internationally and from India's point of view, than China simply claiming Indian citizens as its own or discriminating against Indian citizens from a particular area in the nature of visas issued (Jacob 2011a, 2012).

China and Tibet

For China, Arunachal or NEFA as it was then known had little significance in the early years of the dispute when the attention was on Aksai Chin and as exemplified by its withdrawal from the region in 1962 after ending military operations. A number of reasons have been mooted for what set off the new

Chinese emphasis on the importance of Arunachal Pradesh in the 1980s.[8] There appear to be at least four factors.

> First, Arunachal is rich in mineral, water and timber resources and is therefore important for the Chinese from the point of view of the economic development of the Tibet Autonomous Region (Garver 2001: 109).
>
> Second, the Chinese apparently discovered fresh historical evidence in the 1980s which suggested that links between the Buddhist-majority parts of Arunachal Pradesh and the Tibetan administration in Lhasa were stronger than the Chinese originally believed—Tawang is the birthplace of the 6th Dalai Lama and is believed to have paid taxes[9] to the traditional Tibetan administration in Lhasa. Therefore, Beijing started pressing stronger claims on Arunachal.[10]
>
> Third, in their boundary negotiations during the 1980s, India introduced the idea of a sector-by-sector approach to settling the boundary dispute instead of accepting the so-called 'package deal' of the Chinese. While New Delhi assumed this would allow the two sides to resolve the easier areas of the dispute first before moving to more difficult ones (Singh 2011: 87), Beijing saw this as an opportunity to adopt a maximalist approach in every sector of the boundary dispute.
>
> And fourth, the Chinese central government possibly perceives that stressing its claims of Arunachal Pradesh being part of Tibet territory will somehow reinforce its legitimacy as a defender of Tibetan interests. This is especially germane given that the present Dalai Lama has acknowledged Arunachal to be a part of India (*Times of India* 2008),[11] and given that the Indian government has not prevented him from visiting the disputed territory on various occasions (Roy 2009).

In the context of China's recent troubles in Tibet beginning with the protests in Tibetan areas in March 2008 on the eve of the Beijing Olympics, it is the second and fourth explanations that possibly have the greatest salience. Indeed, the boundary dispute in its basic essence is only a euphemism for the larger problem of the place of Tibet in Sino-Indian relations (Jacob 2011b). In this context, China's travails in Tibet and with Tibetans under its control deserve greater explication.

The Tibetans protests in March 2008 that affected not just the Tibet Autonomous Region (TAR) but also Tibetan areas in the neighbouring provinces of Qinghai, Sichuan, and Gansu, has brought home to Beijing that its policy of relying on the economic development of Tibet is not sufficient to mitigate separatist tendencies in the region. The protests in Tibet, including frequent incidents of self-immolation in 2011, have garnered international attention more for emotive issues such as 'cultural genocide' or for issues of geopolitics rather than the increasingly economic content of Tibetan grievances. So far, Tibet's economic development as envisioned by central government authorities in China has involved huge fiscal transfers and attempts to improve market integration with the rest of the country by means of mega infrastructure projects. While Tibet has been posting double-digit growth over several years now,[12] Tibetans believe that such growth has been largely cornered by Han, including Hui (Han Muslim), migrants. The fact that Han Chinese establishments were specifically targeted during the 2008 protests, show just what Tibetans themselves think of the kind of economic development that they are witnessing (*Economist* 2008).[13]

Despite Beijing's efforts to provide an alternative discourse to that of the Tibetan demand for independence, its Tibet policy has continued to suffer from a Han bias for a number of reasons besides Han chauvinism. For one, economic development requires skills that Tibetans do not usually posses at the current juncture and which slack is taken up by non-Tibetan outsiders. For another, the economic development strategy in Tibet, as in other parts of China, is one of developing economic growth poles from which growth can spill over to the surrounding regions with time. As a result, transport and energy infrastructure are generally geared to cater to larger urban concentrations at the cost of rural areas. These reasons act as both cause and effect where Han migration is concerned and draws complaints from Tibetans who are mostly concentrated in the countryside and who in urban areas have to compete with Han Chinese (Schrei 2002; International Campaign for Tibet 2003).

For China's leaders, the domestic implications of protests and instability in its minority areas are the more serious long-term concern than any international opprobrium. For long, the idea in China has been that economic development and prosperity would make up for constraints on political rights and for other political ills. However, despite several years of sustained economic attention, rising income inequalities and regional disparities are providing additional reasons for political discontent and cultural and ethnic grievances in China's western periphery, including Tibet (Author's interviews 2008b; see also International Campaign for Tibet 2003).

With the Tibetan protests of 2008, the Chinese authorities returned to the familiar tactic of blaming the 'Dalai clique' for fomenting the unrest

(*People's Daily* 2008). More than the economic development of Tibet, it is anybody or any influence threatening the Communist Party of China's (CPC) legitimacy that is Beijing's primary concern. And these influences include not just the Dalai Lama but India too, because it hosts both the Tibetan leader and the Tibetan government-in-exile. India, is thus, viewed with distrust and suspicion by Chinese military and strategic circles.

It is therefore, not surprising that China is particularly sensitive to Indian activities whether of a political or economic nature involving Arunachal or 'southern Tibet' as it calls this area. And given its relative superiority in infrastructure connectivity on its side of the disputed boundary, it is perhaps inevitable that Beijing will use the method of LAC incursions to warn India or at the very least to show hawkish constituents in China that the government and the CPC are being proactive and are capable of defending China's national interests against foreign hands.

At the same time, the Chinese leadership, including its military, is rational enough to understand that China's overall global situation is such that it probably has more to lose by provoking a conflict with India. Indian predictions therefore, of any impending Sino-Indian conflict of whatever scale sanctioned by Chinese central government authorities, are way off the mark and suggest a poor or non-existent understanding of China's national decision-making process and its perceptions of its national interests.

India and Arunachal

For India, the significance of Arunachal post-1962 existed primarily in the military realm and as a reminder of the defeat of 1962. For several decades in fact, physical infrastructure development in Arunachal was first deliberately not undertaken owing to fears of the Ministry of Defence and other central government ministries of providing the Chinese additional advantages in case of another attack (Garver 2001: 99). Today however, infrastructure development is being carried out in response to China's own military modernization and massive infrastructure development in Tibet.

New Delhi while continuing its stress on the military significance of Arunachal is nevertheless, aware that at a time when the chances of major conflict between India and China are diminishing, the importance of Arunachal in the context of a resolution of the boundary dispute lies in building an international case for its retention by India and to counter perceptions of lack of economic and infrastructure development in the state especially when contrasted with Tibet's. Thus, while road infrastructure in Arunachal ostensibly has military implications, they remain thoroughly inadequate for the purpose. Nevertheless, they highlight the fact that it is economic development and international assistance in such construction that is India's main focus.

To push such an agenda, the Indian government has particularly taken to targeting Arunachal's vast natural energy resources, especially hydroelectric power potential,[14] as inducements for domestic investors and foreign multilateral funders.[15] There is no doubt a case to be made for economic development in Arunachal and helping its social, cultural and political institutions to modernize themselves in the age of globalization but the question is whether the Indian government has a well-thought out strategy in place for the purpose.

Larger problems of balancing economic growth with improvement in living standards and sustainable development, including environmental protection and resource utilization, are becoming an issue in Arunachal as they have been for a long time in Tibet. For example, it has been argued that the Indian central government's policies on hydroelectric power do not take into account environmental concerns, including flooding induced by dam construction, of not just ecologically-sensitive areas but also of culturally—and historically—sensitive sites for many of Arunachal's ethnic minorities (Author's interviews 2011). Other massive infrastructure projects in Arunachal such as the Trans-Arunachal Highway have also generated environmental concerns and even concerns about the ability to preserve ethnic identities and cultures as formerly isolated valleys get connected and the influx of 'outsiders' increases.[16] In Arunachal, the desire to preserve ethnic privileges and separation from the outside is a fairly strong trend contending with aspirations for modernization and increased access to the outside world (Author's interviews 2011).[17]

Further, the huge infrastructure development in Arunachal has also led to massive corruption. In a pattern familiar from Tibet, subsidies or development funds are often shared among a patron-client network of political actors (see Naughton 2004: n. 1, 288), including various levels of governments, other institutions and individuals.[18]

Conclusion

From a wider geopolitical perspective, China could well turn belligerent on the boundary dispute for a number of reasons. These include concerns about a potential Indo-US ganging up against China, the possible weakening of Pakistan such that it allows India another opportunity to take advantage as it did in 1971, or fears that a combination of these two events might affect the Chinese hold over Tibet. However, these events are not as likely as most Indians like to think and China itself appears to understand that it will have to deal with India independent of any US- or Pakistan-related concerns and that at the end of the day India's place as an important factor in the Tibet question is undeniable (Jacob 2011b). Considering both the Chinese positions together, it would appear, perhaps somewhat counter-intuitively, that the Chinese are willing to be flexible on the boundary dispute and that its reiterations (such as the claim on the whole of Arunachal Pradesh), retractions (such as on the issue of "settled populations"), apparent hardening of claims (such as on Tawang or in the form of the increasing frequency of LAC incursions) or perceived inconsistencies (such as on visas for Arunachalis) must be viewed only as negotiating tactics.[19]

Meanwhile, the essential purpose of the rather detailed examination of internal developments in Tibet and Arunachal is to draw out broad similarities in the conditions in both regions despite the differing political dispensation in each country. Tibet, in the post-reforms process in China, and Arunachal, in the post-liberalization era in India, have both begun to be shaped in different ways from the rest of their immediate neighbouring provinces/states and certainly from the other Chinese provinces or Indian states further away. These comparisons could also provide indicators at least to Indian authorities how situations can deteriorate in a context of development activities perceived as exploitative, exclusionary or insensitive to local concerns and wishes.[20]

Therefore, no matter when the boundary dispute is resolved, there are larger issues that require focus for both central governments in terms of the wider gamut of their bilateral ties certainly, but also in terms of their policies vis-à-vis their peripheral provinces. India, in particular, given its democratic dispensation and its relative weakness in material capabilities vis-à-vis China has all the greater incentive to improve the quality and application of its democracy in its border states, including Arunachal Pradesh. This would require more transparent processes and greater popular say in development and infrastructure projects than exists in Arunachal, today; this in turn, could prove a model for China-Tibet relations.

Arunachalis often proudly claim that they are the 'first line of defence for India'; indeed, Arunachalis wear their patriotism on their sleeves. It is time now, to consider this 'frontline' as more than a military concept but also one in terms of ideas and norms. Arunachal must also proudly be the 'first line of defence for India's democracy.'

NOTES AND REFERENCES

1. Article VII in the treaty states that "[i]n reaching a boundary settlement, the two sides shall safeguard due interests of their settled populations in the border areas" (Ministry of External Affairs 2005). Chinese Foreign Minister Yang Jiechi told his Indian counterpart Pranab Mukherjee in Hamburg early June 2007 that the 'mere presence' of settled populations did not mean that China was giving up its claims (Samanta 2007).
2. On the eve of Chinese President Hu Jintao's visit to India in November 2006, the Chinese ambassador in India declared on a television channel that his country considered Arunachal Pradesh as part of Chinese territory (*Rediff.com* 2006). Given its timing and given the nature of his job, what was really an unsurprising statement by the envoy of China's position on the boundary dispute was blown out of all proportion by the Indian media. This incident can be said to mark a watershed in terms of the interest taken by the general Indian public in Sino-Indian relations and hence also contributes to the perception of increased violations by the Chinese of the LAC.
3. Former Indian Army Chief, Gen. Deepak Kapoor, stated as much in an interview on television (*Indian Express* 2008).
4. At least on the Indian side, there are several vast areas along the LAC in Aruachal Pradesh that see Indian troop presence only once a year, usually in the form of long-range patrols (Author's interviews 2011).
5. John Garver also talks about China keeping the boundary dispute open as a deliberate way of keeping the India 'sober' vis-à-vis Tibet (Garver 2011: 105-15).
6. I have used this expression elsewhere to suggest that the Chinese might be engaged in such activities not so much to provoke conflict but to create conditions for cooperation (Jacob 2011: 135-39).
7. A question raised in the Rajya Sabha asked specifically if the government was "aware of the facts that China made it clear that it would not issue visas to any official from Arunachal Pradesh and China would continue to issue stapled visas to non-official from Arunachal Pradesh" (Ministry of External Affairs 2011a)
8. John Garver quotes a Chinese journal of international affairs declaring in 1986 that, '[t]he main area of conflict is in the eastern sector,' (Garver 2001: 104).
9. As in the case of many other terms used to describe or explain the nature of the historical relationship between China and Tibet, whether these were really 'taxes' in the modern sense of the word, is debatable.
10. It is perhaps worth remembering that in 1960, a similar development had taken place on the Indian side when the MEA discovered records in British archives in London that suggested India's claims to Aksai Chin were stronger than originally thought. This allowed

Nehru to take a harder line on Aksai Chin after having hitherto expressed doubts about the strength of India's claims (Raghavan 2006: 3889).

11. Earlier in 2003, the Dalai Lama had declared that Tawang and Arunachal Pradesh were part of Tibet.
12. The TAR's GDP has grown at over 12 per cent since 2000, and in 2007, it was 14 per cent or 2 per cent higher than the national average. Rural income too has registered double digit-growth since 2002 (*Economist* 2008: 28).
13. It is also important to note that the 2008 protests had significant numbers of ordinary citizens involved in them, in addition to monks.
14. There are some 170-odd dams of all sizes constructed or currently under construction in Arunachal Pradesh.
15. A cursory look at the list of projects completed and awaiting completion in Northeast India in general shows that a large number of these are related to developing physical infrastructure in the region (North Eastern Council 2005).
16. The primary concern on 'outsiders' relates to the massive influx of labourers from other Indian states for the building of dams and roads. There are however, both intra-ethnic and intra-generational differences of opinion in Arunachal, on these matters (Author's interviews 2011).
17. The desire for cultural preservation appears also to have been appropriated by environmental activists campaigning against mega-hydroelectric projects in the state.
18. In the specific case of Arunachal, however, it has been stated by some social and environmental activists in the state that corruption is "democratic" owing to the small size of the various ethnic groups and the ability, in fact, compulsion, of tribal leaders to distribute the largesse to their ethnic compatriots (Author's interviews 2011).
19. Neville Maxwell, too, has argued that the claim on Tawang was merely a Chinese negotiating ploy (Communication to the author, London, 2 June 2010).
20. Interestingly in 2007, Jaya Bachchan MP in the Rajya Sabha raised a specific question to the External Affairs Minister, Pranab Mukherjee, asking "whether it is a fact that discontent in Arunachal Pradesh has reached such a level that people there are thinking in terms of aligning with China." Mukherjee replied in the negative (Ministry of External Affairs 2007).

REFERENCES

Author's interviews. 2008a. Arunachal Pradesh, December.

Author's interviews. 2008b. With Tibetan activists. New Delhi, March.

Author's interviews. 2011 Arunachal Pradesh, March.

Chaudhury, Nilova Roy. 2008. 'China protests PM visit to Arunachal', *Hindustan Times*. 9 February, http://www.hindustantimes.com/India-news/NewDelhi/China-protests-PM-visit-to-Arunachal/Article1-274630.aspx.

Dasgupta, Saibal. 2012. 'Now, China objects to defence minister AK Antony's Arunachal Pradesh visit', *Times of India*. 25 February, http://articles.timesofindia.indiatimes.com/2012-02-25/india/31100456_1_china-objects-beijing-claims-arunachal-pradesh.

Dholabhai, Nishit. 2007. 'What's new in China visa war? Delhi reply', *Telegraph* (Calcutta). 28 May, http://www.telegraphindia.com/1070528/asp/frontpage/story_7838904.asp.

Economic Times. 2011. 'China says no change in its Arunachal Pradesh policy', 17 January, http://articles.economictimes.indiatimes.com/2011-01-17/news/28432458_1_stapled-visas-weightlifting-grand-prix-indian-immigration-officials.

Economist. 2008. 'Trashing the Beijing Road,' *Economist*, 22-28 March: 26-28.

Ete, Jarjum. 2012. Statement during discussions at the conference, *Voices from the Border: Responses to the Chinese Claim over Arunachal Pradesh*, organized by the ICSSR North Eastern Regional Centre, Shillong and Rajiv Gandhi University, Itanagar, 9 March.

Financial Express. 2007. 'China denies visa to IAS officer from Arunachal', 26 May, http://www.financialexpress.com/news/china-denies-visa-to-ias-officer-from-arunachal/200132/.

Garver, John W. 2001. *Protracted Contest: Sino-Indian Rivalry in the Twentieth Century*, New Delhi: Oxford University Press.

Garver, John W. 2011. 'The Unresolved Sino-Indian Border Dispute: An Interpretation', Special Issue: Revisiting the China-India Border Dispute, *China Report*, 47 (2), May: 105-15.

Indian Express. 2008. 'Chinese incursions due to different perception', 23 February, http://www.expressindia.com/latest-news/Chineseincursions-due-to-different-perception-India/276320/.

Indian Express. 2009a. 'China 'strongly' protests PM's visit to Arunachal!', 13 October, http://www.indianexpress.com/news/china-strongly-protests-pms-visit-to-arunachal/528535/.

Indian Express. 2009b. 'China opposes Dalai Lama's visit to Arunachal', 20 October, http://www.indianexpress.com/news/china-opposes-dalai-lamas-visit-to-arunachal/530979/0.

Indian Express. 2009c. 'Now China objects to Prez Patil's visit to Arunachal', 7 April, http://www.expressindia.com/latest-news/Now-China-objects-to-Prez-Patils-visit-to-Arunachal/444106/0.

International Campaign for Tibet. 2003. 'Crossing the Line: China's Railway to Lhasa', Tibet, Washington, D.C., Amsterdam and Berlin, http://savetibet.de/fileadmin/user_upload/content/berichte/142003RailwayReport.pdf.

Jacob, Jabin T. 2011a. 'Focusing on Arunachal', *New Indian Express*, 26 July, http://expressbuzz.com/opinion/op-ed/focusing-on-arunachal/298127.html.

Jacob, Jabin T. 2011b. 'For a New Kind of 'Forward Policy': Tibet and Sino-Indian Relations', Special Issue: Revisiting the China-India Border Dispute, *China Report*, 47 (2), May: 135-139

Jacob, Jabin T. 2012. 'Make sure you have the new visa for China's walls', *DNA* (Mumbai), 25 January, http://www.dnaindia.com/analysis/column_make-sure-you-have-the-new-visa-for-chinas-walls_1641801.

Kashyap, Samudra Gupta. 2012. 'Stapled visas again, Arunachal players miss China karate event', *Indian Express*, 23 May, http://www.indianexpress.com/news/stapled-visas-again-arunachal-players-miss-china-karate-event/820195/0.

Maxwell, Neville. 2010. Communication to the author, London, 2 June.

Ministry of External Affairs, Government of India. 2005. 'Agreement between the Government of the Republic of India and the Government of the People's Republic of China on the Political Parameters and Guiding Principles for the Settlement of the India-China Boundary Question', 11 April, http://mea.gov.in/treatiesagreement/2005/11ta1104200501.htm.

Ministry of External Affairs, Government of India. 2007. 'Discontent in Arunachal Pradesh', Unstarred Question No. 1904, by Jaya Bachchan, Rajya Sabha. 30 August, http://meaindia.nic.in/mystart.php?id=100513148.

Ministry of External Affairs, Government of India. 2009. 'Funds for projects in Arunachal Pradesh', Unstarred Question No.626, by Prabhat Jha. 9 July, http://meaindia.nic.in/mystart.php?id=100516120.

Ministry of External Affairs, Government of India. 2011a. 'Chinese Visa to people of Arunachal Pradesh', Unstarred Question No.1587, by Kumar Deepak Das, Rajya Sabha. 10 March, http://meaindia.nic.in/mystart.php?id=100517398.

Ministry of External Affairs, Government of India. 2011b. 'Official Spokesperson on stapled

Chinese visa for Indian citizens domiciled in Arunachal Pradesh', 12 January, http://meaindia.nic.in/mystart.php?id=100517058.

Naughton, Barry J. 2004. 'The Western Development Program', in Barry J Naughton and Dali L Yang (eds), *Holding China Together: Diversity and National Integration in the Post-Deng Era*. Cambridge: Cambridge University Press: 253-95.

North Eastern Council. 2005. 'Catalogue of Projects and Schemes of NEC', September, http://necouncil.nic.in/Catalogue%20of%20NEC%20Schemes/Data/index.htm.

People's Daily. 2008. 'Tibet regional gov't: Sabotage in Lhasa masterminded by Dalai clique', 15 March, http://news.xinhuanet.com/english/2008-03/15/content_7793310.htm.

Raghavan, Srinath. 2006. 'Sino-Indian Boundary Dispute, 1948-60: A Reappraisal', *Economic and Political Weekly*, 9 September: 3882-3892.

Rediff.com. 2006. 'Arunachal Pradesh is Our Territory: Chinese Envoy', 14 November, http://www.rediff.com/news/2006/nov/14china.htm.

Rijiju, Kiren. 2012. Statement during discussions at the conference, *Voices from the Border: Responses to the Chinese Claim over Arunachal Pradesh*, organized by the ICSSR North Eastern Regional Centre, Shillong and Rajiv Gandhi University, Itanagar, 9 March.

Roy, Shubhajit. 2009. 'Govt underlines: Dalai Lama free to visit Arunachal', *Indian Express*, 17 October, http://www.expressindia.com/latest-news/Govt-underlines-Dalai-Lama-free-to-visit-Arunachal/530152/.

Samanta, Pranab Dhal. 2007. 'China draws another hardline on Arunachal', *Indian Express*, 6 June, http://www.indianexpress.com/news/china-draws-another-hardline-on-arunachal/32925/0.

Samanta, Pranab Dhal. 2009. 'At ADB, Beijing blocks India's $60-m project for Arunachal', *Indian Express*, 14 April, http://www.indianexpress.com/news/at-adb-beijing-blocks-indias-60m-project-for-arunachal/446709/0.

Schrei, Josh. 2002. 'The Dark Side of China's Western Development Plan', *China Brief*, 2 (7), 28 March, http://www.jamestown.org/programs/chinabrief/single/?tx_ttnews%5Btt_news%5D=3802&tx_ttnews%5BbackPid%5D=192&no_cache=1.

Shukla, Saurabh. 2012. "Arrogant' China raises its pitch for Arunachal Pradesh', *India Today*, 28 January, http://indiatoday.intoday.in/story/sino-indian-boundary-china-arunachal-pradesh/1/170938.html/.

Singh, Zorawar Daulet. 2011. 'After the Hiatus : India-China Border Diplomacy since the 1970s', *China Report*, 47 (2), May: 83-98.

Times of India. 2003. 'Chinese transgressed on LAC in Arunachal: India', 24 July, http://articles.timesofindia.indiatimes.com/2003-07-24/india/27211569_1_lac-chinese-side-chinese-officer.

Times of India. 2008. 'Tawang is part of India: Dalai Lama', 4 June, http://articles.timesofindia.indiatimes.com/2008-06-04/india/27742278_1_tawang-dalai-lama-tibetan-spiritual-leader.

Times of India. 2011a. 'China issues visas to Arunachal karate team', 18 July, http://articles.timesofindia.indiatimes.com/2011-07-18/guwahati/29786447_1_abraham-k-techi-stapled-visas-china-weightlifting-grand-prix.

Times of India. 2011b. 'China issuing 'invalid' stapled visas to Arunachal Pradesh residents', 12 January, http://articles.timesofindia.indiatimes.com/2011-01-12/india/28374355_1_stapled-visas-techi-china-weightlifting-grand-prix.

Chapter 6

China's Territorial Claim on the Indian State of Arunachal Pradesh: The "Centrality of Tibet" and the Balance of Power

Namrata Goswami

The rise of China is one of the most significant political developments of the late 20th and early 21st century. China's economic prosperity, its military modernization, its dominance of manufacturing and commerce, and its growing influence, has caught the imagination of the world like never before. Talk of China is everywhere. Along with this fascination for China, there is also a growing apprehension about the way China will conduct itself in international politics once it is comprehensively powerful. History has been replete with examples of rising powers questioning the status quo in order to improve their own status and prestige in the international system. There are apprehensions that China will challenge the American led international order, and try to shape the international system to its advantage as its power grows.

For India, the rise of China is a challenge. It is a challenge because both countries have primarily dissimilar political systems: China's authoritarianism versus India's democracy. China and India also fought a border war in 1962, which had resulted in India's defeat. India and its military continue to be wary of another 1962 type Chinese attack. Moreover, China continues to claim 90,000 square km of territory in the Northeast of India, which includes the entire state of Arunachal Pradesh (83,743 square km). The gravity of the Sino-Indian border issue and the Chinese claim on Arunachal Pradesh need not be over-emphasized. Maps have been exchanged between India and China on their perception of the Line of Actual Control (LAC), and in 2003, special representatives were appointed by both governments to arrive at an early settlement of the boundary question. In April 2005, both countries signed a pact underlining the broad principles for settlement of the territorial conflict.[1] Despite all these efforts, China continues to assert its claim on Arunachal Pradesh in statements issued by its foreign ministry spokespersons.[2] In June 2009, for the first time ever on a multi-lateral forum, China tried to block India's request for US$ 2.9 billion loan from the Asian Development Bank (ADB) as it included US$ 60 million for flood management, water supply, and sanitation project in Arunachal Pradesh.[3] ADB sources stated that China was unhappy as India had included a project for what they termed as 'disputed territory'.[4] China's move did signal to India that for China, power projection was more critical to arm twist another country over a territorial issue than genuine partnership to resolve it.

It is in this context that this chapter offers an analysis on the Chinese territorial claim on Arunachal Pradesh from the perspective of three significant factors. First, the chapter looks within China's internal dynamics in order to determine the reasons propelling China's aggressive stand on Arunachal Pradesh. Secondly, the chapter analyses the impact of the Tibet factor on China's aggressive posture. And finally, the play of international politics based on the "balance of power" in Asia vindicated by the rise of India and China is factored in to offer a framework to understand the current tensions. Finally, the chapter offers insights on the local Arunachal perspectives on the Chinese territorial claim and outlines the challenges facing the state.

The Issue under Dispute

The Chinese territorial claim on Arunachal Pradesh has increasingly become an issue of grave concern for Indian foreign policy given China's visible assertiveness on the issue in recent years.[5] China's growing influence in world politics, its closed political system, its economic robustness and its military modernization are creating apprehensions about the intentions and capabilities of China. A critical concern with regard to the Chinese claim on Arunachal Pradesh (a state rich in water and mineral resources) is the dependency of the Chinese economy on import of raw materials to sustain its current economic growth.[6] Also, China's territorial claim on Arunachal Pradesh has great symbolic resonance for its legitimacy over Tibet. The 400-years-old monastery in Tawang was the birthplace of the sixth Dalai Lama in the 17th century and is the second largest monastery after Lhasa. It could well be that the 14th Dalai Lama chooses his successor from the Tawang monastery. China, also believes that India makes it possible for the Dalai Lama to travel abroad, and his speeches around the world have kept the Tibetan issue alive and questioned Chinese legitimacy over Tibet.[7] Besides this, Chinese suspicions were aroused when, following the rebellion in Tibet in 1959, the Chinese were verbally attacked by certain Indian leaders, and the mass media. China feared then and still fears now that India might itself become a base for the subversive activities of the Dalai Lama's supporters.[8] Consequently, China's aggressive posture on Arunachal Pradesh to deter the so-called India's Tibet card.

The 2010 Chinese Paper on National Defense reflects these tensions by observing that local and regional conflicts will be a recurring theme in the future.[9] The paper stressed that border security is one of the most important tasks of the People's Liberation Army (PLA) and the Peoples' Liberation Army Air-force (PLAAF) under the supervision of the State Council and Central Military Commission.[10] It is important to note that border security, territorial integrity and social stability are the most recurring themes in the official pronouncements of the Chinese regime.[11]

The chapter will now offer three explanations on why China is getting more aggressive with regard to its posture on Arunachal Pradesh. These are the following: China's internal politics; the Tibet factor; and the balance of power.

(1) China's Internal Politics

Since the communist takeover of China in 1949, the critical challenges for the Chinese Communist Party (CCP) have been regime stability and internal unrest. The stability of the regime and its related legitimacy aspect depended to a large extent on the ideology of communism in the days of Mao Tse Tung. Since 1979, the economic liberalization policies of Deng Xiaoping have taken an upper hand. As a result, the CCP has to now depend on another more entrenched emotional category, nationalism, to legitimize its hold onto power. To be sure, the Chinese conception of nationalism is intertwined with historical beliefs especially its encounter with the West and Japan.[12] Known popularly as the "century of humiliation", China's defeat at the hands of Western powers and Japan deeply affected its notions of dignity and self image. The narrative of the "century of humiliation" starts with China's defeat in the First Opium War, the British acquisition of Hong Kong in 1842, the 19th century unequal treaties with the British and the Japanese, and the war of resistance against the Japanese in the 1930s and 40s.[13] Consequently, an 'aggrieved nationalism' has now developed, which hopes to revert China's status from being a second tier power to global prominence.[14] In an interesting quantitative analysis of China's conception of threats to itself, Gries (2011) found out that in its conceptions of threats from the outside world, China is more wary about humiliation threats than the military balance of power.[15] The study also discovered that feelings of nationalism were higher amongst members of the masses than the party workers.[16] It is therefore important for India to note that Chinese foreign policy choices function not merely within the objective assessment of military balance of power but also the subjective perspective of identity and threat perception. Hence, there is a direct trajectory from nationalism to humiliation to China's foreign policy choices.

The most significant finding about nationalism that this study projects is that, it is not always state funded and conceived. The mass of the people tend to be more nationalistic on issues like Japan and Tibet than the party workers.[17] This aspect played out during the March 2008 Tibetan protests. While the West largely described the official state response against the Tibetan protests and the Dalai Lama as top-down nationalism fed to the Chinese people by the CCP, there was little reporting on the fact that most of the Chinese outrage at the Tibetan protests were coming from the common mass and Chinese diasporas abroad. In fact, most of the outrage on the web decried the Western media as biased, and vehemently asserted that Tibet is an integral part of China. In fact, mass nationalist accused Beijing of being too soft while defending China's core interests.

Deeply connected to nationalism is the Chinese stress on internal stability. Studies on Chinese stability indicate that the economic development of China is the most important principle for the CCP since the 1978 reforms of Deng Xiaoping.[18] In 1992, after witnessing two decades of high economic growth, Deng spelled out his goal for China as the creation of a "socialist market economy with Chinese characteristics".[19] The stress on economics has been paramount leading to almost all leaders after Deng indicating its significance for China's stability and unity. In 1999, Jiang Zemin offered his "three represents" concept which opened up the CCP to private entrepreneur membership as against its earlier confinement to workers and peasants. Hu Jintao also stresses on the significance of economic development as the basis for China's internal unity, strength and stability. Hence, instead of political liberties and rights of every individual citizen, China prioritizes community and social rights and it is the obligation of the state to provide for these rights.[20] Interestingly, the state in China is viewed as the guardian of Chinese civilization and hence enjoys legitimacy and authority. The state is viewed as the parent, the provider, the care-taker based on an optimistic view of human nature unlike the pessimistic view held in Western countries about human nature.[21] As one Chinese historian puts it, "China is...living history. Here almost every event and process happening today is closely related to history, and cannot be explained without taking history into consideration".[22] In China, decision-making with regard to internal and foreign policy is conducted by a very small elite group within the CCP. Consultation, however, occurs on a large scale giving the impression of intra-party democracy.[23] The CCP is responsible for the successful conduct of the economy, acquisition of land for business purposes, bridging the rural-urban divide in income disparity, and political conceptualization of the state.[24] Significantly, due to the lack of political dissent, the CCP does not enjoy the luxury to blame the other for political mishaps, and economic downturn. It is like a corporate state where a few elitist leaders are the decisive actors and are responsible for decisions. The leadership discourages any public debate on larger economic policies, infrastructure, foreign policy issues or governance. Hence, the Chinese state lacks a free press or freedom of expression beyond what is acceptable to the Communist regime.[25] Most institutions in China are designed to restore the legitimacy of the CCP through economic growth especially after Mao's disastrous Cultural Revolution.[26] Hence, from the 1990s onwards, there has been a gradual cutting down of tariff barriers and the enabling of free trade with foreign trade now accounting for about 75 per cent of the GDP.[27] Economic growth has also translated into the modernization of one of the most important institutions of China, the PLA, resulting in international structural fears about the intention of such rapid military modernization.[28]

Uncertainties: Despite the historical continuity of the Chinese state, its civilization strengths and its robust economic growth under the supervision of the CCP, Chinese regime stability has certain inherent uncertainties. Already, the biggest challenge to the regime is equitable growth. The disparity in incomes between urban and rural areas is getting more acute by the day, and the Chinese regime faces the daunting prospect of creating 8 million new jobs every year for its urban population, with an added 15 million new jobs a year for its rural population.[29] Corruption, expropriation of land, and increased taxes has resulted in nearly 100,000 protests a year and if this continues, the regimes' legitimacy is questioned.[30] Coupled with this will be the state's desire to limit dissent leading to tighter control. Significantly, Chinese regime stability critically depends on its ability to keep the current rate of economic growth stable, generate employment, reduce dependence on imports to sustain its economy, and possess an efficient military and police to keep internal law and order. One can perhaps infer about Chinese regime being plausibly insecure about internal dissent given the blocking of news about protests in Egypt from websites in China.[31] It is also uncertain as to how the Chinese regime evolves: would it become more democratic[32] or get even more closed. The issue of factionalism is also a matter of concern within the Chinese regime.

Impact on Chinese Claim on Arunachal Pradesh: If Chinese regime stability is high and it manages its internal contradictions, then China will avoid doing anything seriously aggressive in Arunachal Pradesh. If Chinese regime stability is low, and its internal contradictions get acute, then China will be aggressive with regard to Arunachal Pradesh to divert people's attention from internal instability. Nationalism will also be shored up in order to create the internal environment for right flat form for China's quest to occupy Arunachal Pradesh (they call it southern Tibet).

(2) The Tibet Factor

Tibet is at the heart of China's strategy towards India. The 400 years old Tawang monastery and its importance with regard to Tibetan Buddhism, the presence of a large number of Tibetan refugees in India,[33] the frequent trips to the West by the Dalai Lama from India to talk on the status of Tibet and the international questioning of China's legitimacy over Tibet deeply undercut China's sovereignty over Tibet. The 2008 Tibetan protests, just before the Beijing Olympics, and the spurt of reports on human rights violations in Tibet by China re-opened the Pandora's Box of Chinese insecurity in Tibet.[34] The Dalai Lama's repeated visits to Tawang in Arunachal Pradesh are also viewed as a deliberate attempt by India to undermine China, and keep it on its toes. The Tawang monastery assumes significance for China due to its historical connection with the Lhasa monastery. This historical aspect has been vindicated by interviews in the Tawang monastery where the Lamas recognized the monastery's historical ties with Lhasa monastery until China occupied Tibet in 1951.[35] These ties were based on exchanges of monks and tribute paid in barter to Lhasa. The local administrator in Tawang stated that administrative connectivity also existed between Lhasa and Tawang in the form of judicial and land documents.[36] Locals in Tawang, however, argued that for China to articulate a claim based on history and the conception of Southern Tibet is not only incorrect but deliberate construction of false history. While Tawang had religious and administrative connections with Tibet, no such connection existed with China.[37]

(3) The 'Balance of Power' Perspective

In order to activate the 'balance of power' strategy, a state has to either showcase its military strength to the targeted adversary or use balancing as a tool to vindicate historical territorial claims in a context where the primary goal is to keep the potential peer competitor tied down. In this regard, China continuously asserts that the McMahon Line of 1914 is an imperial British imposition, has no historical basis whatsoever, and has never been accepted by China.[38]

> "China and India are both countries which were long subjected to imperialist aggression. This common experience should have naturally caused China and India to hold an identical view of the above-said historical background and to adopt an attitude of mutual sympathy, mutual understanding, and fairness and reasonableness in dealing with the boundary question. The Chinese government originally thought the Indian government would take such an attitude. Unexpectedly, to the Chinese government, however, the Indian government demanded that the Chinese government give (sic) the British policy of aggression against China's Tibet region as the foundation for the settlement of the Sino-Indian boundary question".[39]

While being aggressive about its territorial claim in the 1950s onwards culminating in a war in 1962 with India, China changed tact and adopted a two track approach towards India once the Cold War ended in 1989 with high level political dialogue, military-to-military contacts, confidence building measures, and bilateral trade,[40] which today stands at US$ 60 billion.[41] China is India's largest trading partner. But lurking behind this cordiality is China's persistent claim on Arunachal Pradesh.[42] Chinese maps show Arunachal

Pradesh as part of the Tibetan Autonomous Region (TAR) and identify it as Southern Tibet.[43] As stated earlier, matters appeared to make some headway with maps exchanged between India and China on their perception of the LAC, and in 2003, special representatives were appointed by both governments to arrive at an early settlement to the boundary question. In April 2005, both countries signed a pact underlining the broad principles for settlement of the territorial conflict.[44]

Disturbingly for India, a sudden shift in China's behavior with regard to Arunachal Pradesh was discernible in 2006. As stated earlier, in November 2006, just days before Chinese Premier Hu Jintao's state visit to India, Chinese Ambassador to India, Sun Yuxi stated that "In our position, the whole of the state of Arunachal Pradesh is Chinese territory. And Tawang is only one of the places in it. We are claiming all of that. That is our position,"[45] In May 2007, China denied visa to Ganesh Koyu, the IAS officer from Arunachal Pradesh and in 2009 blocked India's request for loan from the ADB.[46] In January 2012, China denied visa to Group Captain Mohonto Panging, a senior Indian Air force officer hailing from Arunachal Pradesh, who was to be part of a 30-member Integrated Defence team travelling to China under a bilateral defence exchange programme. Ironically, the visit, starting January 10, was meant to be a Confidence Building Exercise and an offshoot of the Annual Defence Dialogue. India did not cancel the visit per se but instead sent a truncated 15-member military delegation that did not include Mohonto Panging. China again reacted sharply to the visit of the Indian Defence Minister, A K Antony to Arunachal Pradesh when on February 25, 2012, the Chinese foreign ministry spokesperson, Hong Lei, stated that such visits create complications towards resolution of the border dispute.[47]

Why this sudden aggressive Chinese posture against India despite having a mechanism for talks on territorial disputes through the 'Special Representatives' platform? In terms of balance of power, the timing and the context is significant. China is extremely wary of the growing India-US strategic partnership since the end of the Cold War further cemented by the Indo-US Civil Nuclear Deal of July 18, 2005.[48] This was subsequently followed by the signing of the India-US Civil Nuclear Cooperation Agreement on October 8, 2008.[49] Earlier, in 2004, India and the US had signed the "Next Steps in Strategic Partnership (NSSP)", which outlined intensive cooperation in civilian nuclear activities, civilian space programs and high-technology trade, and expanded dialogue on missile defense through a series of reciprocal steps.[50] The strengthening India-US relations is being interpreted by China as motivated by one overarching paradigm: contain China.[51] To Chinese observers, the US is propping up India as a hedge against China.[52] Two important Chinese blogs' entries[53] argued that India's 2009 dispatch of additional 60,000 forces to Arunachal Pradesh was part of a covert Western plan to contain China.[54] The Chinese claim on Arunachal Pradesh is therefore maintained as a bargaining chip.[55]

The Chinese blogs viewed the Chinese military exercise held at Chengdu as a fitting counter to this India-US partnership. China's border forces have also been stationed at Rikaze and east of Yadong and a new airport constructed at Ali with a 4500-meter long runway capable of lifting fighter aircraft and bombers. The *Global Times, the People's Daily*'s English edition (published since April 20, 2009) in an editorial on June 11, 2009, categorically asserted that Arunachal Pradesh is "southern Tibet" and part of China. It interpreted the 60,000 Indian troops in the international border as expressing India's fear and frustration on China's rise since India cannot hope to match China in international influence, national power, and economic scale. India, the editorial argued should give up 'wishful thinking' that China would make compromises on territory.[56] According to a BBC survey of global opinion,[57] 47 per cent of Chinese viewed India negatively as a "dirty, third rate sort of place".[58] Ironically, the current situation between India and China reveals a classic 'prisoner's dilemma' game where two actors are unaware either of the intentions or the capabilities of the other, and hence inadvertently indulge in action that could prove counter-productive in the end.

The Chinese strategic logic of balancing in Arunachal Pradesh is also informed by the continuing 'security dilemma'[59] in India-China relations. This 'security dilemma' arises as China seeks to establish closer ties with countries in South Asia-Indian Ocean region and India is wary of such links.[60] In reality, China has always followed a 'balance of power' approach to counter India. Besides trying to establish itself in South Asia by forging closer ties with Bangladesh, Nepal and Sri Lanka, China has, both covertly and overtly, assisted Pakistan's nuclear and missiles efforts, its military and military-industrial capabilities.[61] The fundamental core in China-Pakistan relations is based on the 'balance of power' logic *vis-à-vis* India. China's foreign policy behavior with Pakistan indicates a belief in China that an estranged relation between India and Pakistan will effectively negate India's ambition for major power status in Asia. Also, the mere existence of the Pakistan threat in India's

Western sector limits India's military capability *vis-à-vis* China in the Eastern sector and strengthens China's ability to realize its territorial claims. For China, the two front war situations for India coupled with the memory of the 1962 defeat of India by China guards against any Indian ambition to counter China in Asia. Hence, Chinese policy makers engage in aggressive territorial posture in Arunachal Pradesh to keep Indian ambitions in check.[62]

The stark aspect of this "security dilemma" came to light last year in an article in the *PLA Daily*, which argued that India's bold military moves in the Eastern sector are motivated by a desire to "contain China" since India views China as a *de facto* competitor in Asia. The *PLA Daily* article further argued that in alliance with the West (read the US), India is aiming to balance China by carrying out the largest military upgrade since 1962 in the Eastern sector. The article was responding to India's decision in October 2011 to deploy the *Brahmos* supersonic cruise missile, which has a flight range of 290 km, in the Eastern sector to strengthen its defence posture *vis-à-vis* China. Also, China is aware that a five-year expansion plan to induct 90,000 more troops and deploy four more divisions in the Eastern sector is also underway. Already, there are 120,000 Indian troops stationed in the Eastern sector, supported by two Sukhoi 30 MKI squadrons from Tezpur in Assam. The distance from Tezpur to Tawang is 345 km and from Tawang to the Line of Actual Control (LAC) is 60 km. The Sukhoi 30 MKI will cover the distance in less than 15 minutes given its cruise speed of 860 mph (1380 km/h) at 32780 ft (10000 m) and 1350 kmph over sea level. Ironically, the PLA article failed to recognize that it was China's own aggressive posture in Arunachal Pradesh coupled with its military modernization in Tibet that had propelled this Indian move.[63]

Internal debates within China have expressed the view that China should teach India a lesson with regard to Arunachal Pradesh. 2012 have been identified as suitable for military action against India. This will assure China's superiority in the regional military balance and teach the US a lesson for cultivating India against China.[64] According to the *Chinese White Paper on Defense 2010*, China aims to win local wars by using information techniques based on the concept of jointness.[65] Given that China is wary of India's desire to become a military power in South Asia-Indian Ocean region,[66] it has upgraded the infrastructure near the international border in Arunachal Pradesh by building an extensive network of roads, railheads, forward airfields, pipelines and logistic hubs for supporting military operations. Intercontinental missiles such as the DF-31 and DF-31A have also been deployed by China at Delingha, North of Tibet. In the border itself, China has deployed "13 Border Defence Regiments, the 52 Mountain Infantry Brigade to protect Southern Qinghai-Tibet region, the 53 Mountain Infantry Brigade to protect the high plateau in the Western sector, the 149th Division of the 13th Group Army in the Eastern Sector and the 61st Division of the 21st Group Army in the Western Sector".[67] Airfields have also been established at Hoping, Pangta and Kong Ka, along with two airfields at Lhasa and an additional four in the region for supporting fighter aircraft and enhance PLA's airlift capability that includes division strength of troops (20,000), brigade air-drops (3,500 troops) and helicopter lift of two battalions.[68] The 2010 US Department of Defense Report to Congress states that China has replaced its old liquid fueled, nuclear capable CSS-3 intermediate range ballistic missile with "more advanced CSS-5 MRBMs" and has vastly improved its border roads in the eastern sector bordering India for PLA movement.[69]

The 2010 China's White Paper on Defense indicates that the PLA now fully operates with the Peoples' Liberation Army Air force (PLAAF) under the concept of jointness based on informationization. This new joint command and control has been operational in the border areas with the induction of new combat troops augmented by modern logistical capacities.[70] Significantly, the PLAAF has transitioned from merely being a support force to an assault force possessing vastly improved helicopters, missile defense and air-strike capabilities. Fiber communication infrastructure has also been installed in border areas to support information based warfare. Under the dual leadership of the State Council and the Central Military Commission (CMC), the PLA is operating in the border areas in coordination with police and civilian authorities.[71] It is clear from the White Paper that the PLA is the core of China military policy in its borders. That apart, the Rapid Reaction Force (RRF) of the PLA will be the first line of defence in the India-China border in case there is a situation of war. As it stands now, RRF has around 200,000 troops, which can be deployed within 24 to 48 hours, whenever a crisis occurs. The RRF comprises of two group armies, nine divisions, three brigades, and seven units, with airlift facilities *via* the IL 76 transport aircraft. Each IL 76 aircraft can take up to 47 tonnes of cargo, and with that kind of capacity, it will be able to deploy the main units quickly to border areas.[72]

The situation, as its stands today in India's Eastern sector, has come full circle. In the first place, China signals aggressive intent with regard to

Arunachal Pradesh. It lays claim to the entire state of Arunachal Pradesh and has been upgrading its military presence in Tibet. As a counter-response, India upgrades its military infrastructure in Arunachal Pradesh to deter plausible Chinese aggression. China views the Indian military upgrade as a response to China's rise in Asia forgetting that its own aggressive posture and military upgrade since 2006 has provoked the Indian response. The consequence of all this is a classic "security dilemma" requiring deft handling as any wrong signaling of intent or offensive military posture from either side could lead to conflict escalation.

The next section offers insights on the local Arunachal perspectives on the Chinese claim.

Local Arunachal Perspectives on the Claim

The perspectives of the various ethnic communities in Arunachal Pradesh on the Chinese claim do not vary widely. Most people interviewed by me across the state stated that the Chinese claim is not validated by history. Interviews in Tawang Monastery, which is perhaps the core reason behind the Chinese claim given its historical linkages with the monastery at Lhasa, indicated that while the monastery had historical links with Lhasa which included religious education, barter trade, and exchange of religious documents, these links with Tibet did not include China. The monks argued that for China to claim that Arunachal Pradesh is Southern Tibet given its historical ties with Tibet is based on a distortion of history as China's occupation over Tibet itself is controversial. Tibet was an autonomous entity historically and while there were religious dialogues between the Lhasa and Tawang monasteries, this did not amount to Tibetan administrative rule in these areas.[73]

The members of Adi, Nishi and Apatani communities stated that China's claim on Arunachal Pradesh is not backed by any historical facts whatsoever. Significantly, these tribes are not Buddhists and hence do not have any religious affiliation with Lhasa.[74] In fact, representatives of the Adi and Galo tribes argued that the main reason why China was aggressive on Arunachal Pradesh was because of the frequent visits of the Dalai Lama to Tawang. They believed that Chinese insecurity over Tibet and the continuous international questioning of its legitimacy there is directly connected to the Dalai Lama's presence in India.[75]

Most interviews in districts like Lower and Upper Siang, Lower and Upper

Subansiri, Tawang and Papum Pare reflected a desire on the part of the local population to improve democratic structures within the state. The local population also supported strengthening of India's defense posture in the border, robust enough to counter China in case it engages in a repeat of 1962. Local politicians 'up the ante" on the Chinese claim state that they fear a "Kargil type" operation by China there.[76]

Three of the main challenges identified by the local people in the state are: governance, riparian issues and border security.[77]

Governance

Most of the districts in Arunachal Pradesh are backward, lack adequate power supply, education facilities, health care, livelihood avenues, and surface communication.[78] Important border districts like Tawang suffer bad road connectivity, a tenuous and risky helicopter service,[79] poor electricity, and absence of good health care.[80] The *Arunachal Pradesh 2005 Human Development Report*[81] identified infrastructure development as one of the key concerns of the state. This was followed up with Prime Minister Manmohan Singh's package of Rs. 24,000 crore in 2009 for building the 1,500 km Trans-Arunachal Pradesh highway.[82] Yet, ground realities continue to be grim with the Border Roads Organization (BRO) stating that it is an arduous task to build two-lane highways in such hilly and inaccessible terrain.[83]

There is a noticeable tendency amongst the local population to compare the high levels of infrastructure in Tibet to that of Arunachal Pradesh. For instance, between 2006 and 2010, China invested 137.8 billion yuan (US $ 20.3 billion) for Tibet's development which included the building of roads connecting 80 per cent of Tibet's villages, providing drinking water to Tibet's population of 2.76 million, free education, new houses, a new Gunsa airport in the Ngari prefecture besides the Gonggar Airport in Lhasa, and a 100,000 kilowatt photovoltaic plant at Ngari. In the first half of 2011, Tibet's GDP grew by 11.2 percent above China's overall GDP growth of 9.3 percent.[84] Also, Tibet registered US $ 836 million of foreign trade in 2010 with a tourism turnover of more that US$ 20 million.[85] Tourism is also supported in Tibet by good connectivity *via* the 1,956 km (Xining to Lhasa) Qinghai-Lhasa railways. In comparison, Arunachal ranked last in the tourism sector amongst the Northeastern states with Meghalaya taking the top spot.[86] Arunachal Pradesh is 90 per cent dependent on Central government funds. In 2010,

India invested around Rs. 5,944 crore (approximately US$ 1.3 billion) under consolidated funds in Arunachal Pradesh.[87] Significantly, the GDP growth rate of Arunachal Pradesh in 2010 was 0.12 per cent.[88] While the state has developed plans to expand the tourist industry, this is not yet supported by reasonably good infrastructure on the ground.[89]

Riparian Issues

Riparian issues are significant in Arunachal Pradesh. Most of the rivers of the state have been identified as possessing enormous potential for hydro-power to the tune of 49,126 megawatt (MW) of electricity.[90] Arunachal Pradesh has signed nearly 103 Memorandum of Understandings (MoUs) with private groups to construct around 103 dam projects in the state.[91] The state has five major river basins, namely, Kameng River Basin, Subansiri River Basin, Siang River Basin, Dibang River Basin, and Lohit River Basin on which 89 major hydro-electric projects are being planned as on date (See Figure I). The largest river is the Siang, which is called the Yarlang Tsangpo in Tibet and the Brahmaputra in Assam.[92] Significantly, local anxieties in Arunachal Pradesh are growing with regard to dams being built by private companies like Jaypee Arunachal Power Construction and Reliance Group. These fears are most apparent with regard to the East Siang River project being built by Jaypee.[93] Locals argue that this project is 'water storage' and not "run of the river" project with a dam height of 86m. Consequently, locals assume that if water overflows during the rainy season and fall from such a height, it will lead to massive flooding downstream and population displacement.[94]

Border Security

Border security is another major issue in Arunachal Pradesh.[95] The shadow of the 1962 India-China war still looms large in the local political discourses.[96] At present, the state of border roads is bad with roads non-existent in some parts near the LAC in the Mechuka area, and landslides obstructing smooth flow of traffic in the Along-Tuting-Gelling and Tawang-Bumla roadways.[97] Most significantly, military intelligence and the local people pointed out that roads on the Tibet side are good and enabled smooth flow of traffic.[98] In terms of defense, India has stepped up its troops' presence in the border[99] but the nature of roads makes logistics and supply lines difficult to maintain. The dangerous air-routes through the mountains also render it difficult for air-traffic to flow in this treacherous mountainous terrain. The Chinese

Map 6.1: Hydro-Electric Power Projects

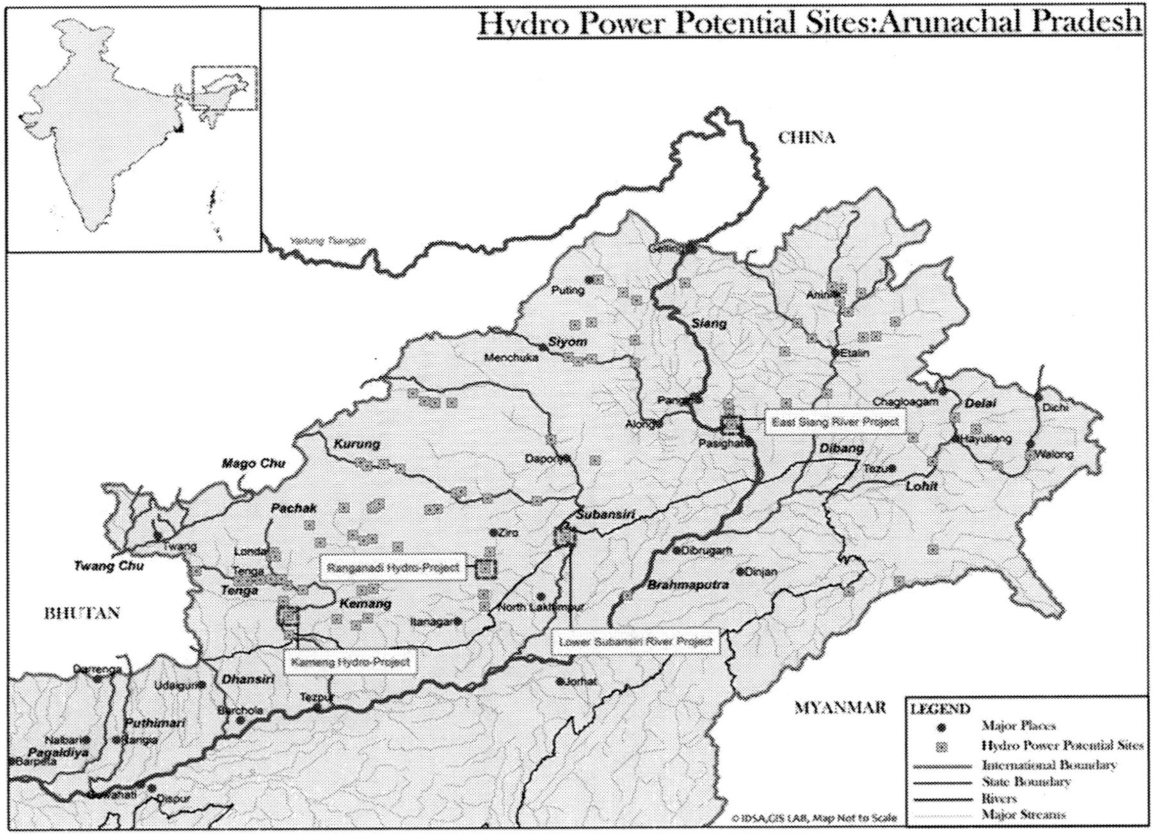

Source: Namrata Goswami.

concept of jointness in its military[100] is not visible in the border areas. Troops stationed in the border areas state that the best way to handle the India-China border issue and the claim on Arunachal Pradesh is through confidence building measures.[101]

Conclusion

In conclusion, it can be stated that the border dispute and territorial claim issue between India and China is not intractable. It can be resolved within the framework of dialogue and negotiation. India must make it clear to China that it will defend its territory by all means, and that coercive diplomacy by China will not work. However, it is in India's interest to find out a viable conflict resolution framework which will ensure settlement of the border dispute in the Eastern sector. This has to be done within a policy of "give and take'. Too much of rigid posturing by both sides will create obstacles. The 2005 framework agreement between India and China offers a broad outline within which the border issue can be resolved.

This contribution was first published as an IDSA Occasional Paper in 2012. Republished with permission from Institute for Defence Studies and Analyses, New Delhi.

NOTES AND REFERENCES

1. For text of 2005 agreement, please see "Text of India-China Agreement", April 11, 2005 accessed at http://www.hinduonnet.com/thehindu/nic/0041/indiachinatxt.htm, accessed on February 10, 2012.
2. "Chinese ire over India border visit", BBC, October 13, 2009 accessed at http://news.bbc.co.uk/2/hi/8304679.stm, accessed on August 16, 2010. Also see Krittivas Mukherjee, "China Opposes Dalai Lama trip to Arunachal Pradesh", Reuters, September 11, 2009 accessed at http://in.reuters.com/article/idINIndia-42388820090911, accessed on November 13, 2009.
3. Pranab Dhal Samanta, "China Strikes Back on Arunachal", *The Indian Express*, September 18, 2009 accessed at http://www.indianexpress.com/news/china-strikes-back-on-arunachal/518626/, accessed on October 19, 2010
4. Raphael Minder, et.al., "China Blocks ADB India Loan Plan", *Financial Times*, April 10, 2009 accessed at http://www.ft.com/cms/s/0/033935c2-25e4-11de-be57-00144feabdc0.html# axzz1QXVRpjF2, accessed on June 28, 2011
5. Namrata Goswami, "China's Aggressive Territorial Claim on the India's Arunachal Pradesh: A Response to Changing Power Dynamics in Asia", *Strategic Analysis*, 35/3, 2011, pp.781-92.
6. China depends on 80 percent import to sustain its economic growth. See "National Bureau of Statistics of China", accessed at http://www.stats.gov.cn/english/, accessed on May 2, 2011.
7. John Garver, "The security dilemma in Sino-Indian relations", India Review, Vol. 1, No.

4 (2002), pp. 1-38.

8. "A Himalayan Rivalry", The Economist, August 19, 2010 accessed at http://www.economist.com/node/16843717, accessed on August 23, 2010.
9. "China National Defense in 2010" Information Office of the State Council, The Peoples' Republic of China, March 2011 accessed at http://news.xinhuanet.com/english2010/china/2011-03/31/c_13806851.htm, accessed on April 24, 2011.
10. *Ibid.*
11. "White Papers of the Government" accessed at http://www.china.org.cn/e-white/index.htm, accessed on April 3, 2011.
12. Peter Hays Gries, *China's New Nationalism: Pride, Politics, and Diplomacy,* University of California Press, Berkeley, 2004, pp. 48-51.
13. Emily Parker, "The Roots of Chinese Nationalism", *The Wall Street Journal,* April 01, 2008 accessed at http://online.wsj.com/article/SB120701186550979029.html, accessed on January 13, 2012.
14. Deng Yong, *China's Struggle for Status: The Realignment of International Relations* Cambridge University Press, Cambridge, 2008.
15. Peter Hays Gries, "Patriotism, Nationalism, and China's US Policy: Structures and Consequences of Chinese National Identity", The China Quarterly, 205, March 2011, pp. 1-17.
16. *Ibid,* p. 13.
17. *Ibid,* pp. 13-14.
18. Chien-min Chao and Bruce J. Dickson, eds., *Remaking the Chinese State Strategies, Society, and Security,* Routledge, London, 2001, pp. 46-75.
19. Prem Shankar Jha, *India & China The Battle Between Soft and Hard Power,* Penguin, New Delhi, 2010, p. 60.
20. Martin Jacques, Martin Jacques, *When China Rules the World The Rise of the Middle Kingdom and the End of the Western World,* Allen Lane, London, 2009, pp. 132-137; David Shambaugh, "China Engages Asia Reshaping the Regional Order", International Security, Vol. 29, No. 3, Winter 2004/2005, pp. 64-99.
21. Jacques, n. 20, pp. 106-9.
22. *Ibid,* p. 197.
23. Gang Lin, "Leadership Transition, Intra-Party Democracy, and Institution Building in China", in Weixing Chen and Yang Zhong, eds., *Leadership in a Changing China,* Palgrave Macmillan, New York, 2005, pp. 37-56.
24. Jha, n.19, pp. 59-94.
25. David Shambaugh, "Containment or Engagement of China? Calculating Beijing's Responses:, International Security", Vol. 21, No. 2, Autumn, 1996, pp. 180-209.
26. For more on this, see Roderick Macfarquhar, ed., *The Politics of China 1949-1989,* Cambridge University Press, Cambridge, 1993.
27. Jacques, n. 20, p. 159.
28. Charles Taylor and Tim Youngs, "China's Military Posture", House of Commons, Research Paper 08/15, February 12, 2008, pp. 1-66.
29. Jacques, n. 20, p. 163. Also see World Bank Office, Beijing, "China Quarterly Update 2009 and 2010" accessed at http://siteresources.worldbank.org/INTCHINA/Resources/318862-1237238982080/CQU_March2009_fullreport.pdf, accessed on May 02, 2011.
30. Jha, n. 19, pp. 59-147.
31. Edward Wong and David Barboza" Wary of Egypt Unrest, China Censors Web", *The New York Times,* January 31, 2011 accessed at http://www.nytimes.com/2011/02/01/world/asia/

01beijing.html, accessed on March 05, 2011.

32. Gang Lin, n. 23.
33. There are about 110,000 Tibetan Refugees in India. See UNHCR "India: Information on Tibetan Refugees and Settlements" accessed at http://www.unhcr.org/cgi-bin/texis/vtx/refworld/rwmain?docid=3f51f90821, accessed on May 02, 2011.
34. Human Rights Watch, "I Saw it with my own eyes Abuses by Chinese Security Forces in Tibet, 2008-2010", New York, 2010, pp. 1-72; Tibetan Centre for Human Rights & Democracy, " Human Rights Situation in Tibet Annual Report 2008", Dharamsala, India, 2009.
35. Interviews with the First and Second Lamas in Tawang Monastery, Tawang, Arunachal Pradesh, March 17-22, 2011.
36. Interview with Deputy Commissioner, Tawang, Arunachal Pradesh, March 17, 2011.
37. Interviews conducted in Mechuka, March 11-13, 2011 and Twang, March 17-22, 2011.
38. The Sino-Indian boundary is divided into the eastern, western, and middle sectors. The eastern sector comprises of Arunachal Pradesh, the western sector includes Ladakh and the middle sector consists of the boundary of Himachal Pradesh and Uttar Pradesh with Tibet. In the eastern sector, the McMahon line was identified through a set of notes between Sir Henry McMahon, the then British Foreign Secretary and the Tibetan delegate, Lonchen Shatra in March, 1914. The Simla Convention of 1914 while recognizing Tibet to be under the suzerainty of China, stated that Outer Tibet was autonomous and there will be no interference in the administration of Outer Tibet by China, which also includes the selection and installation of the Dalai Lama. China views the McMahon line as an imperialist imposition, something which needs to be undone. See Parshotam Mehra, "Northeast Frontier A Documentary Study of the Internecine Rivalry between India, Tibet, and China", Oxford University Press, New Delhi, 1979, pp. 110-139. Also "Contest of the Century", The Economist, August 19, 2010 accessed at http://www.economist.com/node/16846256, accessed on August 23, 2010 and Department of Defense, US, n.15, p. 16.
39. Arthur A. Stahnke, "The Place of International Law in Chinese Strategy and Tactics: The Case of the Sino-Indian Boundary Dispute", The Journal of Asian Studies, 30/1, November 1970, p. 103.
40. Sujit Dutta, "Revisiting China's Claim on Arunachal Pradesh", Strategic Analysis, 32/4, 2008, p.553.
41. Kim Verma, "Indo-China H1 Trade at $30.4 Bn; to Meet $60 Bn Target", July 29, 2010 accessed at http://news.outlookindia.com/item.aspx?688877, accessed on July 31, 2010.
42. Dutta, n. 40, pp. 549-581. Also see "Military and Security Developments Involving the People's Republic of China 2010", Department of Defense, US, 2010 accessed at http://www.defense.gov/pubs/pdfs/2010_CMPR_Final.pdf, accessed on August 17, 2010.
43. Dutta, n. 40, p. 550.
44. For text of 2005 agreement, please see "Text of India-China Agreement", April 11, 2005 accessed at http://www.hinduonnet.com/thehindu/nic/0041/indiachinatxt.htm, accessed on July 7, 2010.
45. "Arunachal Pradesh is our Territory: Chinese Envoy", November 14, 2006 accessed at http://www.rediff.com/news/2006/nov/14china.htm, accessed on August 12, 2010.
46. Sudha Ramachandran, "Chinese Antics have India Fuming", *Asia Times*, May 05, 2009 accessed at http://www.atimes.com/atimes/South_Asia/KE05Df01.html, accessed on June 03, 2010.
47. Saibal Dasgupta, "Now, China objects to defence minister AK Antony's Arunachal Pradesh

Visit", *The Times of India*, February 25, 2012 accessed at http://articles.timesofindia.indiatimes.com/2012-02-25/india/31100456_1_china-objects-beijing-claims-arunachal-pradesh, accessed on March 01, 2012.

48. "Indo-US Joint Statement", July 18, 2005 accessed at http://www.hindu.com/thehindu/nic/indousjoint.htm, accessed on August 22, 2010.
49. "India, United States Sign Historic Civil Nuclear Agreement", India Review, Embassy of India, Washington D.C., November 1, 2008, pp. 1-24.
50. "Joint Press Statement: Next Steps in Strategic Partnership between India and the United States", Embassy of India, Washington D.C., September 17, 2004 accessed at http://www.indianembassy.org/prdetail1148/joint-press-statement-%3A-next-steps-in-strategic-partnership-between-india-and-the-united-states, accessed on August 13, 2010.
51. George Perkovich, "Faulty Promises The U.S.-India Nuclear Deal" Carnegie Endowment for International Peace, September 2005, pp. 1-14.
52. Jeff M. Smith, "India as a US hedge against China", *Asia Times*, August 07, 2008 accessed at http://www.atimes.com/atimes/South_Asia/JH07Df01.html, accessed on August 13, 2010. Also, Ehsan Ahrari, "China's View of US 'lily pad' Strategy", *Asia Times*, August 24, 2004 accessed at http://www.atimes.com/atimes/China/FH24Ad04.html, accessed on August 13, 2010. "A Himalayan Rivalry", The Economist, n. 8.
53. See www.junshi315.cn and in www.warchina.com/n8183c21.aspx, December 11, 2009 analyzed by D S Rajan "China: Nationalistic Blogs Raise New Issues Concerning Sino-Indian Border", South Asia Analysis Group, Paper no. 3562, 24-Dec-2009, accessed at http://www.southasiaanalysis.org/%5Cpapers36%5Cpaper3562.html, accessed on August 12, 2010.
54. Incidentally, estimated Indian troops presence in Arunachal Pradesh is about 120,000. Field observations by the author in Arunachal Pradesh in March 2011.
55. The Economist, Contest of the Century, n.38.
56. B Raman, "Chinese Media Fury over Arunachal Pradesh" South Asia Analysis Group, Paper no.3251, June 12, 2009 accessed at http://www.southasiaanalysis.org/%5Cpapers33%5Cpaper3251.html, accessed on August 4, 2010.
57. See "BBC World Service Poll" accessed at http://news.bbc.co.uk/2/shared/bsp/hi/pdfs/160410bbcwspoll.pdf, accessed on August 17, 2010. 38 per cent of Indian views China negatively.
58. The Economist, "A Himalayan Rivalry", n. 8.
59. For more on this, see John Garver, n.7, pp. 1-38. "Security dilemma arises out of the anarchic nature of the state system. Without a superior power to protect it, each state bears the ultimate responsibility for its own security, for its own survival as a member of the state system. Faced with awesome responsibility, states attempt to expand their power—economically, strategically, and militarily—so as to defend themselves". This makes neighbouring states insecure and hence they prepare for the worst by taking counter-measures to enhance their own power. A common search for security results in a situation in which both powers are less secure. Garver, n,7, p.1
60. Garver, n.7, pp. 3-4.
61. *Ibid*, p. 4. Also see "Contest of the Century", The Economist, n.38.
62. Garver, n. 7, p. 9. See *SIPRI Yearbooks 1981-2009* for "Chinese Arms Transfers to Pakistan" accessed at http://www.sipri.org/databases, accessed on August 19, 2010.
63. Namrata Goswami, "China's Response to India's Military Upgrade in Arunachal Pradesh: A Classic Case of Security Dilemma", November 18, 2011, accessed at http://www.idsa.in/idsacomments/ChinasResponsetoIndiasMilitaryUpgradeinArunachalPradesh_

ngoswami_181111, accessed on March 01, 2012.

64. www.warchina.com/n88582c21.aspx, December 1, 2009 and www.warchina.com/*n8183c21.aspx*, December 9, 2009 analyzed by D S Rajan "China: Nationalistic Blogs Raise New Issues Concerning Sino-Indian Border", *South Asia Analysis Group*, Paper no. 3562, 24-Dec-2009, at http://www.southasiaanalysis.org/%5Cpapers36%5Cpaper3562.html (Accessed on August 12, 2010).
65. "China's National Defense in 2010", Information Office of the State Council, Peoples' Republic of China, March, 2011 accessed at http://news.xinhuanet.com/english2010/china/2011-03/31/c_13806851.htm, accessed on March 23, 2011. Informatization "emphasizes the effects of modern information technology on military decisions and weapons employment cycles". See US Department of Defense Report, "Military and Security Developments Involving the People's Republic of China 2010", Department of Defense, US, 2010 accessed at http://www.defense.gov/pubs/pdfs/2010_CMPR_Final.pdf, accessed on August 17, 2010, p.3.
66. D S Rajan, "How China views India's new defence doctrine", January 07, 2010 accessed at http://news.rediff.com/column/2010/jan/07/how-china-views-indias-new-defence-doctrine.htm
67. Vijay Sakhuja, "Military Buildup Across the Himalayas: A Shaky Balance", *China Brief*, 9 /18 September 10, 2009 accessed at http://www.jamestown.org/programs/chinabrief/single/?tx_ttnews%5Btt_news%5D=35469&tx_ttnews%5BbackPid%5D=25&cHash=255e0ccfe7, accessed on August 14, 2010. For more on China's missiles, see Department of Defense Report, US, n.42, pp. 1-2
68. *Ibid.*
69. Department of Defense Report, US, n.42, p. 38.
70. "China's National Defense in 2010", n. 9.
71. *Ibid.*
72. Park Changee, "North Korean Contingency and Prospects of China's Military Intervention", IIRI Working Paper Series 05, Ilmin International Relation Institute, October 2010, p. 20.
73. Interviews in Tawang Monastery, Tawang, Arunachal Pradesh, March 18-21, 2011.
74. Interviews in Pasighat (Lower Siang district), Daporijo (Upper Subansiri District) and Ziro (Lower Subansiri district), March 13-15, 2011.
75. Interview with Vijay Tamang, Siang Peoples' Union, Pasighat, Arunachal Pradesh, March 07, 2011. Also Mibon, Principle, Holy Child School, Mechuka, Arunachal Pradesh, March 11, 2011.
76. P. Vaidyanathan Iyer, "Arunachal Minister Cautions against 'Kargil-like' Situation", The Indian Express, June 14, 2011 accessed at http://www.indianexpress.com/news/arunachal-minister-cautions-against-kargillike-situation/803346/, accessed on June 15, 2011
77. For more on this, see Namrata Goswami,"China's Claim on Arunachal Pradesh: Local Perspectives", IDSA Issue Brief, July 11, 2011 accessed at http://www.idsa.in/issuebrief/ChinasClaimonArunachalPradesh#.T9RTBLD3IR8, accessed on July 16, 2011.
78. Based on collated interviews with the Deputy Commissioners of various districts in Arunachal Pradesh in March 2011.
79. Two horrific accidents in April 2011, the latter of which killed the Chief Minister of the state are gruesome reminders of lackluster security and safety measures in the state for civilian travel. "Chopper Crash in Arunachal Pradesh killing 17 Tourists", Reuters, April 19, 2011 accessed at http://in.reuters.com/article/2011/04/19/idINIndia-56440220110419, accessed on April 23, 2011. Also see "Arunachal CM killed in Chopper Crash", *The Times*

of India, May 04, 2011 accessed at http://articles.timesofindia.indiatimes.com/2011-05-04/india/29508455_1_chopper-crash-handique-helicopter-crash, accessed on April 25, 2011.

80. Field Visit to Tawang, Arunachal Pradesh, March 19-22, 2011.
81. Arunachal Pradesh Human Development Report 2005 accessed at http://hdr.undp.org/en/reports/national/asiathepacific/india/name,3398,en.html, accessed on March 12, 2011.
82. "PM Announces Time-Frame for Arunachal Projects", Indian Express, October 24, 2009 accessed at http://www.indianexpress.com/news/pm-announces-timeframe-for-arunachal-project/524747/, accessed on December 11, 2011.
83. Interview with S.K. Pandey, Commandant, 44 BRTF, Border Roads Organization, Along, Arunachal Pradesh, March 10, 2011. I also visited the road construction sites along the India-China border in Tato and Mechuka. This is difficult terrain with high mountains and inaccessible terrain.
84. "Hefty Government Investment in Tibet", *China Business News*, May 07, 2011 accessed at http://cnbusinessnews.com/hefty-govt-investment-in-tibet-from-2006-2010/, accessed on May 9, 2011. Also see "World Bank Raises China 2011 GDP forecast, urges tightening", *Reuters*, April 27, 2011 accessed at http://www.reuters.com/article/2011/04/28/china-economy-world-bank-idUSB9E7FE02920110428, accessed on April 30, 2011. For more on Tibet investments, see Chris Devonshire Ellis, "Investing in Tibet, the Roof of the World", China Briefing, April 10, 2010 accessed at http://www.china-briefing.com/news/2010/08/20/investing-in-tibet-%E2%80%93-the-roof-of-the-world.html, accessed on April 13, 2011.
85. "China Economic News in Brief: C919 runway; Tibet foreign trade, Qingdao throughout, Jiangsu agriculture FDI", *China Daily*, February 02, 2011 accessed at http://www.chinadaily.com.cn/xinhua/2011-02-01/content_1706047.html, accessed on February 04, 2011.
86. "Tourism Development Arunachal Pradesh" Ministry of Tourism, Government of India, February 2010 accessed at http://tourism.gov.in/survey/ArunachalPradesh-Feb-10.pdf, accessed on March 12, 2011.
87. For more details see "Arunachal State Budget presented", Arunachal News, March 19, 2011, accessed at http://arunachalnews.com/arunachal-state-budget-presented.html, accessed on May 4, 2011. "Arunachal Pradesh Gazette, Government of Arunachal Pradesh, March 29, 2010 accessed at http://india.gov.in/allimpfrms/allacts/3032.pdf, accessed on April 15, 2011.
88. Also see, Reserve Bank of India "Handbook of Statistics for Indian Economy", accessed at http://www.rbi.org.in/scripts/AnnualPublications.aspx?head=Handbook%20of%20Statistics%20on%20Indian%20Economy, accessed on May 03, 2011.
89. "Tourism Development Arunachal Pradesh" n. 86.
90. For more on hydro-electric projects in Arunachal Pradesh, see "Hydro-Electric Power Policy Arunachal Pradesh", accessed at http://www.arunachalhydro.org.in/pdf/State%20Mega%20Hydro.pdf, accessed on May 12, 2011.
91. Subir Bhaumik, " Damming the Northeast", The Caravan, October 2010 accessed at http://www.caravanmagazine.in/PrintThisStory.aspx?StoryId=513, accessed on June 27, 2011.
92. For more on the Siang, see "Lower Siang Hydro-electric project", accessed at http://agropedialabs.iitk.ac.in/gangapedia/sites/default/files/Lower%20Siang%20Hydroelectric%20Project_Aquatic%20Ecology.pdf, accessed on June 18, 2011.
93. Most of the dams are viewed as storage dams and not run-of the river. Interviews with Peoples' Unions, local academics, activists, civil society and policy makers in East Siang, West Siang, Lower Subansiri and Upper Subansiri districts of Arunachal Pradesh by author,

March 06-17, 2011

94. Interviews with Siang Peoples' Union, Pasighat, March 07, 2011
95. Common view enunciated from interviews by author with policy makers, security personnel, and civil society in Pasighat, Along, Daporiju, Ziro, Tato, Tuting-Gelling area, Mechuka, and Hari village in Ziro, and Tawang in Arunachal Pradesh, March 2011.
96. Interview with political officers from the 1962 period; village elders in Mechuka affected by the Chinese aggression in 1962.
97. Field visit by author to these areas in March 2011.
98. Interview with military intelligence, Tawang, Arunachal Pradesh, March 17, 2011.
99. Estimated strength at around 120, 000 troops stationed in Arunachal Pradesh. This also includes the 2009 announcement by Governor of Arunachal Pradesh J J Singh about two new mountain divisions raised for Arunachal comprising 25,000 to 30,000 each. Interviews with military personnel in Arunachal Pradesh, March 2011. Air support envisioned from Tezpur, Assam, where there around two Sukhoi 30 MK1 squadrons. The distance from Tezpur to the Tawang is 345 kms and from Tawang to LAC is around 60 kms. A fighter jet Sukhoi 30 MK1 will cover the distance to over 16,500ft in less than 15 minutes given its cruise speed: 860 mph (1380 km/h) at 32780 ft (10000 m) and 1350 km ph over sea level. Based on field inputs in Tawang, March 2011. Field observation by author, March 2011. Also see Indian Military.org Arunachal Pradesh accessed at http://www.indian-military.org/tag/arunachal%20pradesh.html, accessed on March 13, 2011. "India decides to step up military presence in Arunachal Pradesh", Arunachal News, accessed at http://arunachalnews.com/india-decides-to-step-up-military-presence-in-arunachal.html, accessed on March 12, 2011.
100. "China National Defense in 2010" Information Office of the State Council, The Peoples' Republic of China, March 2011 accesssed at http://news.xinhuanet.com/english2010/china/2011-03/31/c_13806851.htm, accessed on April 24, 2011.
101. Interview with 190 Mountain Brigade stationed in Tawang for securing the LAC on the Indian side at Bumla, March 19, 2011. Also interview with army division stationed at Along for LAC security, Tuting-Gelling, Arunachal Pradesh, March 09, 2011. Interview with Indo-Tibetan Border Police, Ziro, Arunachal Pradesh, March 15, 2011

Chapter 7

Border Dispute in the Eastern Sector: Why Does China Refute the McMahon Line?

Gomar Basar

Introduction

China and India have already fought a war in 1962 primarily over the border issue. Both China and India have been striving for long to negotiate for an amicable solution to the vexed border dispute. The two giants share a land border that spans over 4000 km and has traditionally been divided into three sectors: the Eastern Sector, the Middle Sector and the Western Sector. The Western Sector involves the dispute over an area of approximately 38,000 sq km in the Aksai Chin area which India claims as part of Ladakh in Jammu Kashmir and China claims as part of Xinjiang and Tibet. Besides this, Pakistan has ceded another 5,180 sq km area of Indian territory of Pakistan occupied Kashmir (POK) to China. The Middle Sector involves a dispute over various points between the Tibet-Kashmir-Himachal Pradesh border junction and Nepal-Tibet-Uttarakhand border junction. The Eastern Sector involves dispute over a total area of 90,000 sq km. According to China, this area is composed of Tibet's three districts of Monyul, Loyul and lower Zayul (Map 7.1), while India administers this area and refers it as Arunachal Pradesh, formerly the North-East Frontier Agency (NEFA).[1]

At present the Line of Actual Control agreed upon by both sides, by and large, conforms to the McMahon line. But China regularly questions the validity of this line and resorts to different coercive diplomatic measures to highlight its reservations. The primary tactics used by China inter alia are:

(1) Showing State of Arunachal Pradesh in their maps and search engines websites as Southern Tibet.
(2) Issuing stapled visa to the inhabitants of Arunachal Pradesh.
(3) Blocking Asian Development Bank loan to state of Arunachal Pradesh.

This chapter addresses the problems associated with the claims and counter claims in Eastern Sector since the Simla Convention of 1914. The primary impetus would be on the colonial shortcomings in establishing a mutually agreed boundary.

The Historical Legacy

The origin of the border dispute between India and China dates back to British colonial rule in India. Before this time, the border was a common frontier and nobody knew for certain as to where exactly India ends and China begins. The entire China-India boundary was never been formally delimited by any mutually accepted treaty. The present boundary took shape on the basis of each other's administrative jurisdiction that evolved in post-colonial period.[2] It becomes imperative to understand the gradual ascendance of the events which necessitated these developments since early part of 19th century.

Early British Policies towards the Eastern Sector

Prior to the advent of British in Assam plains and the Chinese forces in Tibet, the Eastern Sector (Arunachal Pradesh) was *terra incognita* and remained cut off from the rest of the world. The tribes living in foothills gradually came in contact with the people living in the plains only after the 16th century when the Ahom rule was established.[3] The outbreak of the First Anglo-Burmese War (1824-1826) in Assam ushered in the beginning of the modern era for North East Frontier Tract (now Arunachal Pradesh). It was in the wake of subsequent signing of the treaty of Yandabo in 1826 that the British came in contact with the hill tribes of Arunachal Pradesh. This event had led the colonial British administration to deal with the hill tribes of Arunachal Pradesh as the tribesmen had age-old claims over the plains of Assam bordering hills and they were accustomed to collect taxes in the form of posa (political bribery) annually from the Assamese inhabitants since the Ahom times.[4] As

Sketch Map 7.1 : Showing Arunachal Pradesh with Tibetan Names

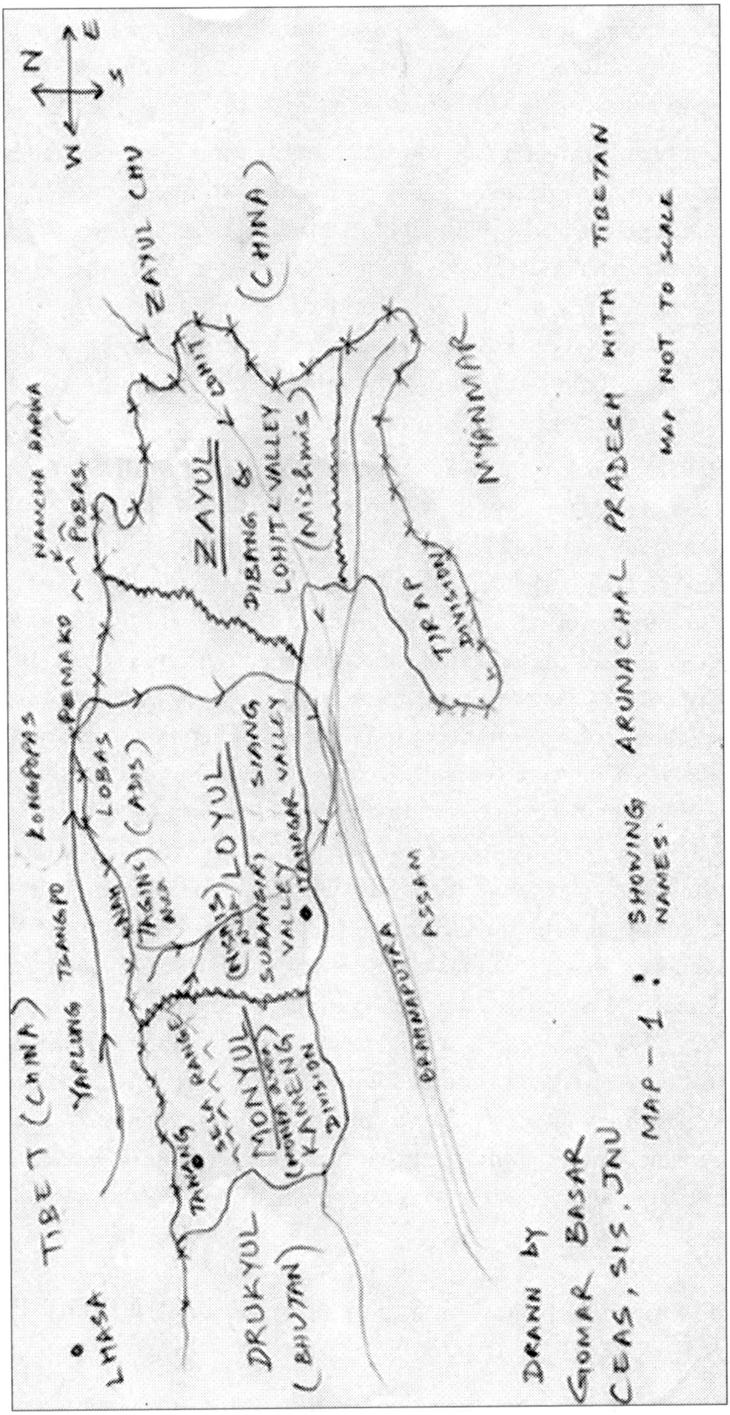

Britishers started expanding their area of influence, they found out that the territories in the foothills were extremely rich in natural resources with tea bushes, coal and petroleum abundantly found in upper Assam.

The initial British policy towards the tribes was to protect the British tea plantations and extraction of coal, petroleum and forest wealth without any confrontation with the tribesmen of Arunachal Pradesh. Therefore, the British continued the payment of posa to the hill tribes of Arunachal Pradesh as in the days of the Ahom. This British policy of appeasement failed in the due course of time as the tribesmen carried on feudatory incursions into the plains of Assam with a view to punish the refractory subjects who refused to pay taxes defying the age-old tradition.

So in order to ensure security and to protect the British interests in Assam, the inner line regulation act was passed in 1873. According to this act, a restriction line was laid down to regulate intercourse between the British subjects and with the hill tribesmen. However, the Britishers were also interested in the bright economic prospects of the resources in the hills like timber, wax and mineral deposits and so on. Alongside the British also contemplated to explore a trade route to China through North East Frontier to gain monopoly of opium trade in China.[5] Therefore, the British wanted to exercise an indirect control over the tribal areas. Hence, the undefined and ambiguous territory beyond the inner line was to be kept with them through some imaginary line. So they came with outer line which was not fixed to suit their colonial interests. This outer line was gradually extended in due course of time which became the contested boundary between India and China at present. China's claim of Arunachal Pradesh (southern flank of the Himalaya) is basically on this ground, i.e. British India administration was limited to inner line and the areas beyond this line were under Tibetan administration and hence constitute the Chinese territory. Chinese claim rests on the fact that Tibet exercised some administrative control over Tawang Dzong which was predominantly Monpa dominated areas. The influence was exercised through Tawang Monastery which was established in the 17th century.[6]

China's forward policy in Assam Himalaya (Mishmi hills) under Zhao Erfeng (1910-12)

Since the signing of the Boxer protocol in 1901, the Qing dynasty feared that Mongolia and Tibet would be reduced to Russian and British protectorates. Therefore before its extinction in 1911, the Qing court strove to restore its old prestige in Mongolia and Tibet. It intended to annex the eastern part of Tibet by military might and create separate provinces under direct Chinese control as they did in the case of Xinjiang in 1884.[7] So in order to actualize their objectives Chinese pursued a twofold policy: First, to assert control over Tibet by sending high officials, and second, to intensify the policy of annexation and colonization adopted by the governor-generals or border commissioners of Sichuan and Yunnan. To affect the first strategy Zhang Yintang, the first ever Han Chinese official was appointed as the High commissioner of Tibet, who conducted an investigation tour of Tibet in the wake of the Anglo-Chinese agreement of 1906. Zhang intentionally entered Chumbi Valley that was under the British occupation, to demonstrate that the Chinese had replaced the British as the major force in Central Tibet.[8]

During the last decade of the Qing Dynasty, Cen Chunxuan (1902-03), Xi Liang (1903-07) and especially the Zhao brothers (1907-11), Zhao Erxun and Zhao Erfeng, successive governor-generals of Sichuan, exercised considerable influence in Qing politics and initiated the campaign of military conquest of Tibet with the intention of putting it under the direct administration of the Qing government.

Face to face

By the beginning of the seventies of the 19th century, the economy of Assam had become promising and trade and industry had a good start. But, the prospect of Assam's economy depended on the capacity of the British administration to maintain law and order as well as to check any influence from other foreign power. As a result, their loose political control towards the hill tribes came to an end by 1910, as the political development in Tibet was fast changing with wide implications for the British India. After the 1910 military intervention in Lhasa, the Chinese forces occupied Zayul in August 1910 and neighboring Pome in the eastern Tibet in 1911, thus coming in contact with the Assam hills (Mishmi hills) to their south. From the Chinese point of view, these areas like eastern Tibet could be used for Chinese settlers and moreover connected to Yunnan and Tibet by a route that could be an alternative to the Sichuan and Lhasa route. After occupying Zayul, Zhao Erfeng (border affairs commissioner) started to exert Chinese influence on the neighboring tribes of Mishmi hills. It was reported that over one thousand

Chinese troops had entered Rima and were collecting taxes. The British were alarmed with this development and tried to consolidate their position in Assam Himalayas (Dafla hills, Abor hills, Mishmi hills, etc.) which until then was not under any effective British control. These events were reported by the Mishmi people to the British as they regarded themselves to be British subject.[9]

The most disturbing news for the British during that time was that the Chinese authorities in Peking was contemplating to dispatch troops down the Siang river towards the Adi country (Siang Valley) which if carried out might have led to Chinese claim over the Siang Valley. Such Chinese activities could not be allowed and now the British Assam itself was threatened by the Chinese move.[10] The Sino-phobia compelled the British to adopt a forward policy and to assess the extent of Chinese influence on the hill tribes of North Eastern Frontier. The British Government dispatched the parties of geological survey like 'Mishmi Mission' under W.C.M. Dundas to survey the Lohit Valley (now Lohit, Anjaw, Lower Dibang and Dibang Valley districts), 'Abor Mission' under A.H.W. Bentick, Deputy Commissioner of Lakhimpur to survey the Siang Valley and 'Miri Mission' under G.C. Kerwood, Sub-Divisional Officer, Lakhimpur to survey entire Subansiri Valley and Kameng Valley up to Bhutan in order to fix primarily a boundary between British India and Tibet (China) and also to check the Russian designs in Tibet. As Britishers bide time so as to pursue the border issue with China, succession of events took place. The Xinhai revolution in 1911 overthrew the Manchus (Qing emperor was forced to abdicate in favour of the republic). This was soon followed by Tibetan revolt and killing of Zhao Erfeng and subsequent declaration of independence after forcing the Chinese armies out from Tibetan areas. However, Tibetan independence was not recognized by Great Britain due to existing treaties with China but their policy towards Tibet changed and they started planning to redefine the status of Tibet to its own advantage.

Simla Conference and McMahon Line

Simla conference was held in 1914. British India was represented by Henry McMahon, Chinese by Chen Ivan, and Tibet by Lonchen Shatra. The conference was held under very difficult circumstances as each participant had their own set of interests which were contradictory to each other. The Chinese nationalist Government was very weak to repudiate any attempt by British from initiating a conference to discuss on its internal subjects, as they continued to claim that Tibet in its entirety was part of China. Tibet on the other hand wanted to assert independence from China. While Britishers planned to create a buffer between China and the British dominions along the Himalayan states like that of one existing between Russia and China with Mongolia as the buffer.

The Tibetan, the British and the Chinese delegates initialed the Simla Convention document of the 27th of April, 1914. Liu Xuecheng has argued in his article, "Look beyond the Sino-Indian Border Dispute" that Ivan Chen initialled the document without the consent of the Chinese government under threat and pressure from McMahon. Further he argued that Ivan Chen had the clear understanding that 'to initial and to sign are two different actions', and that his initials would not bind his government, whose views he would immediately seek. On July 3rd, 1914, China repudiated the action of Ivan Chen, both his signature and his acquiescence to any form of Tibetan autonomy. That same day, upon the Chinese refusal to ratify the document, Henry McMahon and the Tibetan representative, Lonchen Shatra, initialed a second convention where McMahon line was shown on map.[11] Liu has argued further that there were actually two parallel conferences at Simla, the tripartite conference focusing on the division of Tibet, and a secret one, keeping Chen Ivan out of the negotiations on the Indian-Tibetan boundary. In early 1914, Henry McMahon and Lonchen Shatra secretly negotiated on the division of Tibet and the boundary between Assam and Tibet as a package deal. An agreement was reached through a secret exchange of notes in Delhi on March 24 and 25, 1914. He opined that McMahon line was outcome of this agreement. He further argued that as far as the objective of the Simla conference was concerned, it clearly failed. The McMahon Line was not even accepted by the British-Indian government. After the Simla conference, from 1914 to 1935, on the official maps published by the Survey of India, the McMahon Line was not penned; instead it was the Outer Line along the foothills of the Himalayas that was shown. The Tibetan authorities continued to exercise administrative jurisdiction in the tribal areas as they did before. The Simla conference therefore went down in history as an unaccomplished cause. But here it is noteworthy to mention that Xuecheng is considering inner line as the outer line which was established in 1873 by inner line regulation. Outer line was a notional line which the Britishers extended as per their need and administrative convenience.

Nevertheless in spite of China's argument on the validity of Simla conference outcome, the major lasting legacy of the Simla convention was the McMahon line, which British India considered as the boundary with China. The present border between India and China also follows the same alignment with the highest watershed in the eastern Himalayas as the boundary which was outlined in the maps during the Simla convention. But there are certainly several issues which have not been properly addressed during the Simla convention and this has accentuated to a major issue between India and China.

Challenges of Geography and Culture

The findings of the survey and exploration works conducted by the British officials were utilized in the drawing of the McMahon line on the maps at a scale of 1:38,00,000 which is very small to provide the exact and accurate location on the ground. Consequently there are geographical limitations to the exact location of the boundaries. Moreover, the boundary was never delimited on the ground. As such there is no clear boundary as one degree variation in the map means several miles variation on the ground.[12] Due to these anomalies there is misunderstanding between Indian and Chinese soldiers. Often each side complains of intrusions which are actually due to misperception about the boundary on the both sides.

Also, as the McMahon Line follows the principle of highest watershed then it is worth referring here that the highest watershed in the Mishmi hills should be the Kangri Garpo mountain range (see Map 7.2). But the actual line which was drawn at the Simla Convention restricts it to lesser ranges much below Rima (Zayul). Though India never claims this territory but previously it was under British India as the local inhabitants (Mishmis) consider themselves to be British subjects. That is why they reported to the British government about the Chinese occupation of the Zayul area in 1911. Noteworthy Mishmis residing in the Chinese side are known as Deng. They have not been included as ethnic minority group in China till now.[13] On the other hand Chinese troops under Zhao Erfeng visited the Zayul Valley for the first time only in 1910-11. Perhaps their stay was for a very short duration as before they could establish any administrative mechanism, the Qing dynasty was overthrown in 1911. Also, Indian explorer Pandit Kishen Singh surveyed the Zayul in 1882.[14] This can be stressed upon as Chinese are trying to validate their claim over Aksai Chin on the ground that in 1890, Chinese surveyor Li Yuanbing, surveyed the entire Aksai Chin.[15]

Sketch Map 7.2: Showing Disputed Territories Between India and China

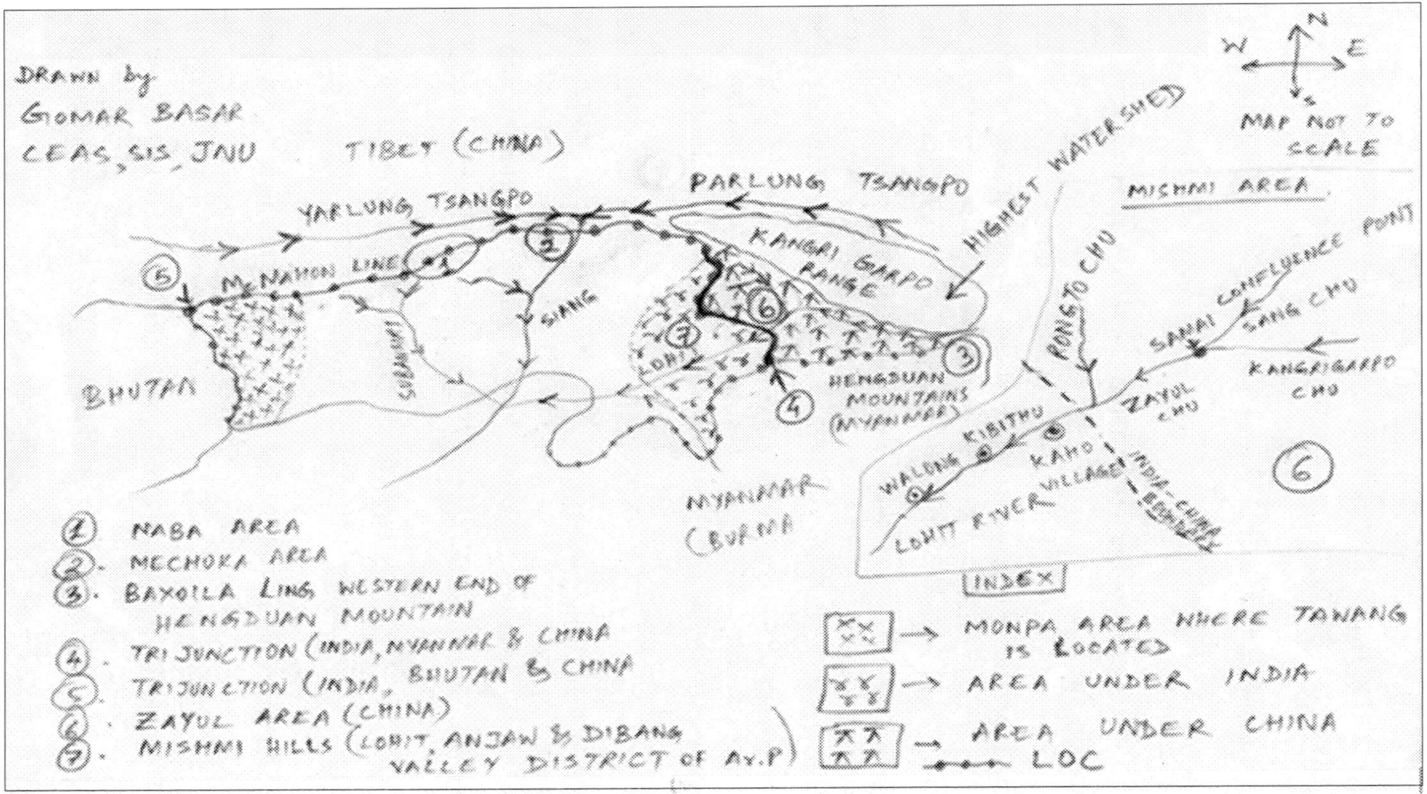

If China can claim the territories of India on the basis of Buddhist cultural influence like that of Tawang then the areas which are inhabitated by Lhobas in Tibet like Nah, Bagni, Yidu, Tagin and Bokar can also be claimed by India. So on the cultural (ethnic) basis; border can be redrawn as it has been done by China with Myanmar in their border treaty of 1964.[16]

Conclusion

The present dispute over the boundary between India and China has been primarily due to the historical blunders which British India committed during its rule in India. Firstly, British India created an inner line within Assam and left the territories beyond it as outer line without bringing it under its administration. Thus the area was open for any powerful country to occupy. As Tibet was never powerful enough, in due course of time, China could strengthen its hold in Tibet. This happened in the Zayul area in 1911. Secondly, the British organized the Simla Convention and created the controversial McMahon Line. This line was not accepted by China. Thirdly, Tibetan issue was embroiled into the boundary row because of which China finds it difficult to accept the McMahon Line as the legitimate boundary because acceptance of this line would mean accepting the Tibetan Independence. Fourthly, the McMahon line was drawn on map without considering geographical and cultural factors in the right earnest. Also the watershed principle, the avowed basis on which McMahon line is said to have drawn, was not followed strictly. The boundary line was drawn much below near Walong and thereby leaving the vast territory of Zayul which otherwise would have been in India as Kangri garpo range is the highest watershed in the region.

Nevertheless, the Simla Convention has been a watershed in creating a boundary defining the territorial extent of both India and China. Although there are disagreements on the actual positions on the ground, however, the present Line of Control by and large follows the alignment as earmarked during the Simla Convention barring few areas of disputes such as Tawang. In recent times China is claiming areas beyond the high water line because of her other interests, not because of any historical record. Perhaps the situation surrounding the border between India and China is simply a matter of realpolitik. The historical, geographical and cultural factors are of limited significance.

NOTES AND REFERENCES

1. Liu Xuecheng, *Look Beyond the Sino-Indian Border Dispute,* China Report 47: 2 (2011), pp. 147–58.
2. Ibid.
3. Pandey, Deepak, *History of Arunachal Pradesh (Earliest times to 1972 A.D),* Pasighat, 1997, pp. 278-392.
4. Lego N, *Modern History of Arunachal Pradesh (1825-2006),* Itanagar, 2006, pp. 106-107.
5. Ibid.
6. Discussion with Dibyesh Anand near Lohit Hostel JNU. He is currently Reader (Associate Professor) in International Relations, Centre for the Study of Democracy, Department of Politics and IR, University of Westminster, Wells Street, London, UK.
7. B.R. Deepak, *India & China 1904-2004; A Century of Peace and Conflict,* Manak Publications, Delhi, 2005, p. 198.
8. Ibid.
9. Bhutani, V.C., *Sources of Frontier Studies: The North East Frontier of India, China Report* 1988, 24: 299, p. 303.
10. Ibid.
11. Ibid.
12. As discussed by Prof. Srikanth Kondapalli during M Phil second semester class lecture at CEAS, JNU session 2011-12.
13. Youyi Huang, Dreams of Snow land, Foreign Language Press, Beijing, 2005, pp. 73
14. Nakamura Tamotsu, "Kangri Garpo range in South Asia",www.jac.or.jp/english/jan/vol1 p. 3.
15. Ibid.
16. International boundary study No.42 November 30, 1964 Country codes: (BM-CH). Office of the Geographer and Global Issues, Bureau of intelligence and research, Dept. of State, USA.

Chapter 8

Chinese Claims over Arunachal Pradesh: A Foot Soldier's Perspective

J.R. Mukherjee

Introduction

Chinese claim in the Eastern Sector of about 90,000 sq km encompasses most of Arunachal, to the North of the River Brahmaputra, with the general limits of the claim being the area South of the McMahon Line up to the approximate alignment of the Arunachal-Assam border (except in Lohit District).[1] The Chinese refer this entire area as South Eastern Tibet and have so depicted it on their general map.[2] Notwithstanding the above, the Chinese are yet to officially intimate their exact claims in the Eastern Sector to the Government of India.

Whilst I have no intention of going into the historical details of the Chinese and our claim and counter-claim, I would confine myself to my personal perceptions of lesser known aspects, based on a fairly intimate knowledge of most of the claimed area and the people of Arunachal over many years—from being an avid China watcher over the last 48 years and my own assessment with a view to assist in attempts at problem resolution to the Sino Indian Border Dispute in this region.

The Claims in a Nutshell

The Chinese claim that the entire area of Arunachal is part of Tibet (South Eastern Tibet) and that as they have ruled undisturbed over Tibet for over

700 years and as for which they consider Tibet an integral part of China, this entire area in Arunachal Pradesh belongs to them.[3] The Chinese, in addition to claiming the entire area, state that they do not recognise the McMahon Line (in spite of the fact that after the 1962 war they themselves withdrew behind the line).[4]

India's claim is backed by recorded history such as the Ahom Burunjis' accounts of the British historians, and the Tibetans and local folklores.[5]

The Tibetan Counter-claims in a Nutshell

The Tibetan Government in exile, on the other hand, counters this claim by giving evidence that Tibet was a totally independent state since 1913 and prior to that, it had, at no stage in history, been a part of the Middle Kingdom. Their relationship with the Mongolian rulers was one of priest and patron—the Tibetans being the priests of Mongol Royal families and hence they had their political patronage from time to time. There was never any structured Chinese rule or formal suzerainty over Tibet.[6]

Indian Claims

In 1914, the Tibetan Government signed the *Simla Accord* with the British rulers of India demarcating the border between India and Tibet and called the same the McMahon Line, which is later claimed by India, being the inheriting state, and which has been accepted by the Tibetan Government in Exile.[7]

Further, the people of Arunachal have always been fiercely independent—Tibet also at no stage had control over Arunachal—the interaction with Tibet was invariably only cultural and commercial in limited areas where the common point was Buddhism (which in fact had originally spread from India).[8]

Specific Chinese Claims related to McMahon Line

Even though the Chinese do not recognise the McMahon Line, on grounds of it being a colonial imposition, interactions with them indicate that they differ at places with the interpretation of the alignment of the McMahon Line on ground, as it has only been delineated on a large scale map. There is also an issue of interpretation of the Line of Actual Control (LAC). Whilst India interprets the LAC to be based on the limits of control over areas physically held by the opposing forces of India and China, the Chinese interpretation is different. The Chinese interpretation whilst not elaborated by them in recent years, as far as the Eastern Sector is concerned appears to be related to their interpretation on ground of the alignment of the McMahon Line. This analysis is drawn from a letter from Chou En Lai to Pundit Nehru in the sixties wherein he refers to forward location of troops of both sides as in 1959.[9] The LAC is again referred to by the Chinese in their comments to the Colombo Proposals of December 1962 in the same light. This needs to be specified by them in concrete geographical terms and an understanding between both Governments needs to be reached on the subject.[10] However, from the above facts, if presumed correctly, and from discussions with the Chinese and analysis of general maps, the following areas of further disputes emerge in relation to the Eastern Sector:

- *The location of the Sino-Indian (Sikkim)-Bhutan tri-junction of the border*—the according to the Chinese claim is to be further South than that claimed by India. The effect of this claim is, if accepted, that it would facilitate the Chinese out flanking existing Indian defences in Sikkim and Bhutanese defences.
- *The location of the Sino-Indian (Arunachal)-Bhutanese tri-junction*—here again the Chinese claim it to be much farther South of what India claims the alignment to be, that is in the Tawang Sector. Hence the Chinese claim to the Thagla Ridge, Khinzemane and other locations in the sector and parallel claims in Eastern Bhutan.
- *Consequent to the dispute regarding the tri-junction at both locations the Chinese also have claims to Bhutanese territory*—defence of Bhutan is an Indian responsibility and a Treaty obligation which has a bearing on the defence of both Sikkim and Arunachal.
- *In the Subansiri sector*, the Chinese claim that Longju is in Tibet and not in India.
- *In the Anini/Dembuen sector* claims are still to emerge, there being little Chinese activity as opposed to the other sectors currently, as they are extremely rugged and difficult.
- *In the Dibang Sector*, China claims a fairly large area which is currently under Indian occupation.
- *In the Lohit Sector the claim is in relation to the Sino-Indian (Arunachal)-Myanmar Tri-junction*—here again the Chinese claim it to be much farther South. If that is accepted, the entire area up to

Walong would fall in Chinese Tibet.

- In addition to the above, I have no doubt that if and when LAC physical demarcation is done between the two countries more disputes are bound to arise.
- There are in addition, other major differences in both the Western (Aksai Chin in Ladakh) and Central Sectors (Barahoti-Uttaranchal).

Other Specific Chinese Claims

Notwithstanding the dispute related to the LAC and the general claim to most of Arunachal as mentioned earlier, China has indicated certain specific claims based on the alleged direct Tibetan control, religious or cultural affinity over specific areas in Arunachal including the Tawang Tracts in the past. These are as follows:

- The significance of the claim to Tawang Tracts, which corresponds to Tawang and West Kameng districts of Arunachal Pradesh, lies in the fact that the Sixth Dalai Lama was born in Tawang in the 17th century, and the Tawang Tract with Se La as the dividing line is claimed to be the fiefdom of the Dzongpens (high officials) of the Tsona district in Tibet. Notwithstanding the specific Chinese claim to this huge chunk of Western Arunachal, like a dagger jutting down to the Assam plains, it must be noted that the entire Tawang Tract being South of the McMahon Line is clearly part of India; and that the Tibetan Government in Exile and the Dalai Lama have publically declared that Tawang is part of India.[11]
- In the Subansiri Valley, Asafila, an all-weather pass (just South of the alignment of the Indian perception of the McMahon Line) along the Subansiri River, and the Portrang Ridge, which is part of the Takpasiri Mountain, also known as the "Crystal Mountain", are considered holy not only by the Tibetans, but also by the Monpas and Tagins of Arunachal Pradesh. It has been a place of pilgrimage since time immemorial and is again specifically claimed by China. The ridge in the shape of a dagger, ending opposite Taksing, is bounded by the Subansiri River and the Yume Chu stream. A pilgrimage used to be undertaken every 12 years, starting from Chosam in Tibet. It followed the Tsari Chu Valley till its junction with the Subansiri River and then up the Subansiri River Valley till Taksing. From here the route turned north up the Ridge or along

the Yume Chu. The pilgrimage would end at the holy Yume Gompa (monastery). This longer version of pilgrimage, called "Ringkor", was undertaken over a three-month period and several thousand pilgrims passed on this route, staying in caves and bamboo shelters, which were called "Tsukang". The local people stocked these shelters with food and wood. The pilgrims passed through this challenging and difficult route. The Tagins, who live in the Upper Subansiri Valley, were paid yearly tribute by the Tibetans of Longju and a special large tribute to help this pilgrimage every year. Today, the pilgrimage has stopped as the McMahon Line divides Takpasiri and the valleys of Arunachal Pradesh. In case this area is granted to China it would compromise Indian positions along both the streams including Taksing.[12]

- Longju, which is South of the McMahon Line has been illegally occupied by the Chinese including the area of the Bisa Cane Bridge, a few km to its South, on grounds that the population is of Tibetan descent.[13]
- In the Siang Sector, the entire Siyom Valley including Mechuka and Manigong, and from the border up to Gelling in the Siang Valley, have some population of Tibetan origin similar to Tawang and are again considered by the Chinese to be fiefdoms of Tibet. The Gompa at Mechuka is also considered a holy shrine by the people of Monpa and Tibetan origin as well as by the Adis and also the Sikhs as it is claimed to have been a resting place of Guru Nanak during his visit to Tibet. In fact a Gurudwara has also been set up near Nishangong enroute to Yorlung, which was also considered to have been a resting place of the Guru Nanak and has other folklore attached to this shrine. I have little doubt that these areas would ultimately be specifically claimed by the Chinese on the same grounds as Tawang. Here again, the Tibetans accept these areas to be part of India and are well South of the McMahon Line.
- The Dibang Sector has been the roughest and least inhabited area of Arunachal Pradesh, where on account of cartographic errors the Chinese have specific claim to a fairly large area.
- In the Lohit Sector, the specific Chinese claim, besides the claim up to Walong, is to the Dichu pass itself on the watershed—this is disputed by India and is under Indian occupation. In addition, the

area from the border up to Walong also has some population who are of Tibetan origin and would in all probability be claimed by them at some stage on the lines of Tawang.

Chinese proposals for Dispute Resolution

Notwithstanding all the above specific claims, China, in 1959 and even till as late as recent times, was prepared to do a swap of the Western Sector known as Aksai Chin, which is strategically more important to her, with the Eastern Sector (Arunachal Pradesh) to resolve the dispute.[14] This was, however, not agreed to by the Indian Government on grounds that China had illegally occupied the Western Sector and that such an act amounted to gifting Indian territory, which they were not authorised to do as also public sentiment was strongly against it.[15]

A series of meetings between officials of both countries were held with no worthwhile results. Notwithstanding this, consequent to meetings between the Heads of State of both countries, several treaties related to ensuring Peace and Tranquillity along the borders have been signed between the two countries, starting with the Border Peace and Tranquillity Agreement in 1993 and the last having been signed in 2005, relations actually improved and in the early period of 2003-04 it was felt a resolution of the dispute was in sight. In 2005, the meeting between Wen Jiabao and Manmohan Singh was seen as a turning point in relations wherein it was agreed to resolve the border dispute without displacing settled populations.[16]

Deterioration of Relations

Unfortunately from 2006 onwards, just prior to Hu's visit to India when China reactivated her claim to Arunachal—something which had been more or less accepted as settled—there were also increased intrusions and relations between both countries deteriorated, with China becoming more belligerent and assertive with consequent strong reiteration of its entire claim. Visas to Arunachalees were also denied on grounds that Arunachal is considered to be a part of China. Accusations were also levied in relation to Kashmir and PLA troops inducted into POK. This state of affairs continued till the Lhasa rebellion of 2008 and incidents thereafter. Both countries reportedly reinforced deployment on the borders, China speeded up her emphasis on building warlike infrastructure in Tibet towards the Indian Border, so did India. India commenced raising two additional divisions of troops besides reinforcing Air

Force deployments in the North East. It is only during a meeting at Hun Hua, when Manmohan Singh and Wen Jiabao met on the sidelines of the Asia Pacific Economic Conference that the two premiers reached an understanding—the two countries would have a strategic partnership for regional peace and stability and narrow differences on the border issue through dialogue based on political principles already agreed upon.[17] Both Premiers agreed to ensure peace and stability in border areas and to improve cooperation on bilateral issues. Consequently relations between India and China improved.[18]

Unfortunately incidents in Tibet reoccurred in 2010, 2011 and even in 2012 resulting in tension and strained relations frequently notwithstanding the new agreement reached with reference to handling border issues.[19]

Reasons for Non-Resolution

The question is, why is this occurring? It is important to find out the reasons for the same as herein lay the path to the resolution of the dispute. In my opinion, the roots of the problem remain largely unchanged since 1962—the same reasons for which China attacked India.

As it was then and also now, the issue remains primarily Tibet and the Chinese failure to quell the Tibetan rebellion and assimilate the Tibetans into their mainstream civilisation and politics. In the pre-1962 war, support to the Tibetan rebellion in the form of training and provision of arms to the rebels from Indian soil was considered by China to be an act of war. Consequently, current Indian support to the Tibetans and relations with the Dalai Lama and the Tibetan refugees is looked upon with great suspicion.[20]

It must not be forgotten that in 1909, the then Dalai Lama fled to India when the Manchus invaded Tibet and he returned to Tibet after three years to push the Chinese out of Tibet and declare Tibet independent. This is an issue that China has never forgotten till date particularly since India has given asylum to the Dalai Lama and more than a lakh of Tibetans. India has also allowed the Tibetans to set up a Government in Exile at Dharamsala. India had also upgraded the level of dealing with the Tibetans from Under Secretary to that of a Joint Secretary and arranged meetings between the Dalai Lama and the Indian Foreign Secretary. As far as China was concerned, this amounted to recognition to the Tibetan Government in Exile—a blatantly anti-Chinese act. India also allowed Tibetan leaders to have a conclave at

Dharmsala, where the Chinese claim the rebellion was plotted. According to Chinese claims, it is from here that the pro-independence movement and rebellion in Tibet is being plotted. The rebellion is being claimed to have been coordinated over mobile phones and the Internet. All these have led the Chinese to raise anti-India rhetoric, particularly when the Indian PM was to visit Arunachal, and reversed her previous agreement with India for resolution of the dispute without disturbing settled populations—an extremely retrograde step.[21] Even recently the Tibetan rebellion in Sinchuan and demonstrations at Delhi over the meeting between the Special Representatives of the two countries for the border talks last month have been reported adversely by China. China has now declared Tibet a Core Interest for full assimilation into the Middle Kingdom.

It must also be understood that the Dalai Lama has demanded autonomy for not only Tibet but also all old Tibetan areas of greater Tibet surrounding it that includes a major part of Yunnan and adjacent regions—almost a quarter of China. The terms of autonomy demanded almost amount to independence—a status similar to what Bhutan enjoyed with India in the past.[22] With all the international attention Tibet is now getting, China is frantic and is prepared to go to any lengths to prevent Tibet breaking away. This includes going to war if such an occasion arises.

China's support to Pakistan and her recent induction of large numbers of the PLA into the Northern Areas, thereby posing a further threat to the Western Sector and J & K and her re-iteration of her claims to Arunachal, are now major irritants.[23]

These have been further compounded by a perception that India is joining hands with the US, Japan, Australia, Vietnam, Philippines and South East Asia in a perceived strategic alliance against China—this perception started with the Indo-US Nuclear deal and strategic partnership. The issue of India now looking East and becoming a trade and scarce natural resources competitor, disputes over the Chinese damming and thinking of diverting Ganga and Brahmaputra River waters in Tibet, have also complicated relations in spite of the surge in Sino-Indian trade.[24] There is also the fact that it is only recently being perceived that Arunachal has tremendous natural resources that China is now eyeing. All these issues have only added fuel to the fire in relations between India and China.

Chinese realisation of their growing confidence, internationally enhanced position, economic and military strength and that of the shifting of balance of power from the West to the East is also a recent phenomenon which has given the Chinese added belligerency and assertiveness.[25]

Conclusion

In reality, the reasons for China's recent assertiveness over Arunachal and other issues therefore lie primarily within the scope of China's and India's foreign and economic policies—it is these policies that need to be harmonised to the extent feasible so as to avoid belligerency and to facilitate resolution of the dispute. In case we wish a resolution of the border dispute, I am strongly of the view that we would need to rein in the activities of the Tibetans in this country and for that matter the Dalai Lama. We would also have to be prepared to follow a policy of give and take in reference to the actual dispute whilst bearing in mind the sentiment of our own people, particularly those of Arunachal. Notwithstanding these foreign policy measures, we must be in a position to negotiate with China from a position of strength, i.e. military strength, adequate border infrastructure to support countermeasures against China; and most importantly by developing Arunachal adequately.

NOTES AND REFERENCES

1. P.B. Sinha, A.A. Athale, S.N. Prasad, eds., *History of the Conflict with China, 1962*, History Division, Ministry of Defence, Government of India, New Delhi, 1992; Also see, Neville Maxwell, *India's China War,* Penguin Books, London, 1972
2. Global Times, *Peoples Daily*, 3 October 2009 and repeatedly before and thereafter; Google maps; Texas University, Perry-Casteneda Library, accessed at http://www.lib.utexas.edu/maps/china.html,
3. Xu Yan, *True history of the Sino-Indian Border War*, Cosmos Books Ltd., Hong Kong, 1993, p. 28, 29-30, 50, 53.
4. Transcript of audio tapes of seminar and speech by Dr Wang Yiwei, Associate professor at Fudan University Shanghai, when he spoke to Indian experts on China on the invitation of the Observer Research Foundation on India China relations in 2007 at Delhi.
5. John W. Garver, *The Protracted Contest: Sino-Indian Rivalry in the Twentieth Century,* University of Washington Press, Seattle, WA, 2001
6. Julia Famularo, "Spinning the Wheel: Policy Implications of the Dalai Lama's Reincarnation", Project 2049 Institute Paper, January 30, 2012. Also see, Tsering Sakya, *The Dragon in the Land of Snows: A History of Modern Tibet since 1947*, Columbia University Press, New York, 1999.
7. Sinha, n. 1
8. Proceedings of a Seminar on "India-China Border Dispute: Way Ahead" held at CLAWS on 11 August 2010.
9. B.N. Mullik, *My Years with Nehru-The Chinese Betrayal,* Allied Publishers, New Delhi, 1971.

10. Steven Hoffmann, *India and the China Crisis*, University of California Press, Berkeley, 1990.
11. "Tawang is part of India–Dalai Lama", *Times of India*, 4 June 2008, accessed at http://articles.timesofindia.indiatimes.com/2008-06-04/india/27742278_1_tawang-dalai-lama-tibetan-spiritual-leader, accessed on June 14, 2013.
12. Yan, n. 3.
13. Sinha, n. 1
14 Zhou Enlaiwaijiaowenxuan (Diplomatic documents of Zhou Enlai), Zhongyangwenxianchubanshe, Beijing, 1990, p. 268-276.
15. Chinese Foreign Ministry spokesperson, Liu Weimin, in response to a press question concerning the reference made by Gen J J Singh to the need for New Delhi to 'move away' from its non-negotiable stand on the border issue, made no direct reply, but said, "the two nations should seek a package solution to the border issue through negotiation based on the spirit of peace, friendship, equality-based consultation, mutual respect and mutual understanding" (Beijing, 21 April 2012). The use of the term 'package solution' could be a significant pointer to the Chinese thinking on what 'give and take' should be.
16. Srikanth Kondapalli, "India-China: Protracted talks, contested sovereignties", rediff news, January 2012, accessed at http://www.rediff.com/news/column/india-china-protracted-talks-contested-sovereignties/20120119.htm, accessed on June 14, 2013.
17. Prem Shankar Jha, "A Shadow over the Himalayas: India's Tibet Problem," AsiaVisions 28, May 2010 accessed at www.ifri.org/downloads/av28psjha.pdf, accessed on June 14, 2013.
18. Kondapalli, n. 15
19. "China: Tibetan-consciousness movement spreads", B Raman, October 25, 2011, accessed at http://ramanstrategicanalysis.blogspot.in/2011/10/china-tibetan-consciousness-movement.html, accessed on June 14, 2013
20. Jha, n. 16.
21. *Ibid.*
22. *Ibid.*
23. China: The Unfolding Asia-Pacific Strategy, By D.S. Rajan, October 2011, Mr D.S. Rajan, is Director, Chennai Centre for China Studies, Chennai, India, his presentation at an international seminar on " India in the Asian Century: Expectations and Implications," organised by the Centre for Southeast Asian & Pacific Studies, Sri Venkateswara University, Tirupati, India, on 7 September 2011.
24. Claude Arpi, "China's water war with India," June 25, 2011 accessed at http://www.vigilonline.com/index.php?option=com_content&task=view&id=1568&Itemid=72 accessed on June 14, 2013; also see, Brahma Chellaney, "China's Dam Frenzy"December 2, 2011 at http://www.project-syndicate.org/commentary/china-s-dam-frenzy, accessed on June 14, 2013.
25. Michael D. Swaine, "China's Assertive Behavior-Part One: On 'Core Interests'," *China Leadership Monitor*, No. 34, Winter 2011.

Chapter 9

Tibet, Monyul and Loyul: An Overview of Relations in the Ganden Potrang Era

Mathew Alkester

Communist China's claim to the territory of Arunachal Pradesh rests on the notion that it was under Tibet's control up to the mid-20th century. This paper will briefly review the history of Tibet's relations with these regions in the modern era, that is, to say, since the formation of the modern Tibetan and Bhutanese states in the mid-17th century, when a new geopolitical configuration took shape in the region. This requires drawing a basic distinction between Monyul, which belonged to the Tibetan world, and the rest of what is now Arunachal, what the Tibetans call Loyul.

Monyul

When I say it was part of the Tibetan world, I am talking about an area encompassing the entire Tibetan plateau, and a few lower-altitude pockets on its fringes, inhabited by speakers of Tibetan dialects, with a common written language, followers of Vajrayana Buddhism, who have distinct regional identities but share a common historical and cultural heritage. The people of Monyul are as distinct from central Tibetans as any other group within this mosaic, in terms of their language, dress and food. Before the 14th century, they appeared as an independent local kingdom holding sway over both northern and southern neighbours.[1] Nonetheless, like the neighbouring kingdoms and fiefdoms in what is now Bhutan, and indeed other trans-

Himalayan states, these rulers traced their origins to the imperial Tibetan dynasty.[2] Unlike other peripheral Tibetan peoples, however, the Monpa came under the direct rule of the modern Tibetan state, soon after its formation in 1642.

The pre-modern relations between Tibet and Monyul are beyond the scope of this paper, but it should be noted that the term "Mon" is a basic ethno-regional marker in Tibetan culture, with a wide variety of meanings. In modern colloquial language it refers to the cis-Himalayan region in general, and in particular, the region that is now Bhutan. This region, including Monyul, was traditionally known as "Lho Mon" ('southern Mon'). After the formation of the Drukpa state, the term 'Monpa' in Tibetan came to refer specifically to the inhabitants of Monyul.

Monyul, as we now know it, came into being through the military campaigns waged by the new Ganden Potrang state against the emerging Drukpa state from 1644 to 1714. Its people were determined to defend their land against their neighbours to the West, and resisted incorporation into Drukyul. They did this by forging an alliance with Ganden Potrang and its Mongol army, which used Drukpa aggression against Monyul as a main pretext for military intervention.[3] The chief protagonist of this alliance, like many of the charismatic political figures of that time, was a Lama, named Lodro Gyatso, a native of the Merak region (now in the Tashigang district of Bhutan) that his forces attempted and failed to hold against the Drukpa. As it is well known, Merak Lama was a personal disciple of the 5th Dalai Lama, the spiritual founder of Ganden Potrang, and a champion of the Gelukpa school (now the state religion of Tibet) in a region otherwise dominated by the Drukpa, Nyingma and Bon schools. He founded the great monastery of Tawang as a bastion of the Gelukpa political and religious order in a hostile frontier region, on the authorisation of the Lhasa government. The 5th Dalai Lama's 1680 edict sealed the annexation of the Tawang tract to the northern stretch of Monyul governed from Tsona Dzong, forming a single administrative region under the joint political and religious authority of the Tsona Dzongpon and Merak Lama.[4] The fact that a child from Tawang was recognized as the reincarnation of the 5th Dalai Lama (d.1682) is typical of the religio-political links traditionally cultivated by Tibetan rulers to promote the cohesion of peripheral regions with the centre.

By the time Ganden Potrang rule was re-established in 1728 (after a period of civil war in central Tibet), its wars with Bhutan were over, and the southern part of Monyul, now known as the 'three valleys below the passes' (La 'og yul gsum), formally constituted as part of the administrative structure. Tawang monastery was a state institution under the Drepung monastery in Lhasa, which appointed senior functionaries. A group of 'six joint officials' (rTa dbang drug 'brel) consisting of the lay and monastic officials appointed to Tsona Dzong and Tawang monastery were charged with the collection of tax and administration of justice in the territory. This arrangement continued into the 20th century.[5]

The economic significance of Monyul to the Tibetan state was substantial. It was the only rice-growing region under its administration, and the state enforced a monopoly, organising an annual barter of Tibetan salt for Monpa rice from Tsona Dzong (mTsho sna 'bras sgrub). Indeed, Tsona Dzong was not a historic centre of administration in the region, and seems to have gained importance with the regulation of Monpa tax and trade in the Ganden Potrang era. In addition to grain and butter, Monpa tax obligations included a range of exotic produce ranging from spices, medicinal plants, honey and musk to wild animal skins, dye, paper, bamboo products and the birch wood tablets used for Tibetan block printing. The hardwood timbers used to furnish the Potala palace were procured as a tax from this region. It was, in other words, a cornucopia, and onerous tax obligations dominate accounts of Monpa-Tibetan relations before 1950. There were also corvee labour obligations and the monk tax commanded by Tawang monastery. The main beneficiaries of the tax revenue from Tawang monastery's estates were the Loseling college of Drepung monastery and the Yiktsang Lekhung, or palace secretariat.

More research is needed to precisely define the rights and obligations of the Tawang Monpa under the Tibetan state, and there is little documentation available. On the available evidence, I would tend to characterise Tawang as an internal colony of the Lhasa government, in view of its onerous tax obligations, minimal participation or influence in central decision making and the tenuous cohabitation of local rulers with central authority, particularly the Sat Raja of southern Monyul, or Kalaktang. It should be appreciated, however, that these features were common to most of the territory ruled by Ganden Potrang, which did little for any of its lay subjects beyond collecting tax and administering justice.

Tawang's territorial status with respect to the British government of Assam after 1825 is adequately demonstrated by the 1843 annexation of the Kariapara Duar (known to the Tibetans as 'Ambartala' = Amratulla), the

Geling Raja affair of 1852 and the implementation of the 1873 Bengal Eastern Frontier regulation.[6] The 'Officials' report' on the 1960 border talks is the fullest presentation of the Indian position on China's claim to Arunachal that have been made public.[7] It must be said that the arguments put forward in this document with respect to Monyul lack any sense of history, or even logic. We cannot examine them in detail here,[8] but the gist is that Tibet's jurisdiction in Monyul was merely ecclesiastical, that the officials deputed to the territory from Lhasa were exclusively concerned with the monastery, and collected not taxes but religious donations. This seems disingenuous at the least: the modern Tibetan state was founded on the principle of combined secular and religious authority, and the majority of productive land was parcelled out to ecclesiastical or private estates that managed them on the state's behalf in return for enforcing its writ.

The Officials' Report claims that Tibetan presence was limited to monastic and private estates within a territory under Indian administration, but that applies to the situation after 1914, for these were the conditions on which Tibet ceded Tawang, not to the situation beforehand. If Tawang had really come under British administration before that, why did Geling Raja have to flee to the plains to escape Tibetan jurisdiction, why were Tibetan officials involved in approving the 1873 Inner Line boundary between Assam and Monyul, and why indeed was it necessary for British India to negotiate the McMahon Line at all, if it already administered the territory?

The argument that Monyul belonged to British India before 1914 is misconceived and unhelpful. In adopting this position, the GOI stooped to the cynical thuggery of its opponent and ceded some of the factual and moral high ground that it otherwise holds in this dispute. India's claim to Monyul goes back to the bilateral agreement of 1914, and stands only if India will affirm that the Tibetan government with which it reached that agreement was a legitimate and independent authority competent to sign treaties with its neighbours. India of course failed to affirm this in 1950 when the PLA invaded Tibet and moved China's frontiers up to the Himalayas. That failure seems to have undermined its moral and intellectual coherence in handling the consequent dispute over the border.

The issue has become even more critical lately, since the British government renounced its last diplomatic ties with Tibet. The United Kingdom was the only UN member to stop short of recognizing China's sovereignty, and to use the formula 'suzerainty' instead, because imperial

Britain was unique in having signed treaties and conducted diplomatic and military relations with an independent Tibet. With a statement by foreign minister David Miliband on October 29, 2008, Britain renounced this position as an "anachronism" and a "colonial legacy". The thinking behind this extraordinary concession is unclear, but we do know that China's foreign ministry was looking very pleased with itself indeed that day.

One implication of this bureaucratic rewriting of history would be that Britain no longer recognizes the validity of the McMahon line, because it is a colonial-era treaty and therefore an "anachronism". I am not aware that India has clarified the position with the British government, at least in public.[9]

I very much hope not to be misunderstood. I am not suggesting that independent India should have relinquished its claim to Monyul, nor that it should have declared support for Tibetan independence. I am simply suggesting that it has been a mistake to appease a relentless bully in the hope of buying peace, to renounce India's legitimate interests in Tibet in the naive hope of securing a cooperative relationship with China.

Loyul

The remaining 95 per cent or so of what is now Arunachal Pradesh was known to Tibetans as Loyul, or 'land of the Lopa'. 'Lopa', a generic term for the non-Tibetan peoples of these hills, means 'savage' and corresponds with a Tibetan Buddhist stereotype of warlike, semi-naked, omnivorous forest dwellers who know no religion and do not understand killing to be a sin. Loyul was outside Tibet's borders, political and cultural, and no major routes to India passed through the region, but local Tibetan states like Char-yul and Po-yul naturally conducted relations with their immediate southern neighbours and even had Lopa subjects. Tibetan inhabitants of all regions bordering Loyul had regular and by many accounts amicable trade relations with the Lopa. They were keen consumers of Tibetan salt, ironware and weaponry, woolen cloth and grain, while the Tibetans were interested in medicinal herbs and forest products, wild animal skins and, it seems, slaves. There is, in other words, a long history of Lopa-Tibetan relations, including traditionally accepted frontiers in some places. My intention here is limited to the proposition that, with one small exception, Ganden Potrang had no powers of administration or taxation in Loyul south of the McMahon line.

The small exception is the Pachakshiri enclave, now known as Mechuka, in West Siang, a valley colonized by Tibetans apparently from the early 18th century. At that time, some leading Lamas of the Nyingma school were articulating the cult of 'Pemako', a 'hidden valley' in upper Siang where the faithful might take refuge in times of war and persecution. From that time, Tibetan Buddhist migrants, some from Eastern Bhutan and Monyul, others from the border region or from Kham (Eastern Tibet) began to settle in the region, fleeing excessive taxation and oppressive rule or following the prophecies of the Lamas. Their settlements were hard won against the hostility of the Lopa whose land this was, and of the unfamiliar climate, but grew somewhat with successive migrations from Kham in the early 20th century.

The Pachakshiri valley, more accessible from Tibet and at higher altitude, was successfully colonized by refugees from the Kaliyug in the same period. Nothing much is known of the episode any more, but we can speculate that the Lamas who led their followers to sanctuary here had undertaken to convert the local Ramo and Bokar people to Buddhism. This was no paradise either, however, for by the 19th century it had become, by virtue of its Tibetan/ Buddhist population, a lucrative addition to the Gachak estate in Kongpo, which collected a variety of agricultural and forest produce in tax, and administered justice through local headmen. This estate was granted by the Tibetan government to Lhalu, one of the senior noble families in Lhasa, in about 1860. Tax collection continued there until Indian administration was established in the early 1950s.[10]

Pemako, the Tibetan name for the uppermost reach of the Siang valley, was more involved with Tibet than other regions of Loyul due to historic relations between the Adi inhabitants and the neighbouring kingdom of Po-yul, and these relations quickened with the arrival of Tibetan-speaking migrants since the 18th century. Again, we cannot go into the complex history of inter-community relations in the region here, but it should be noted that traditional alliances and balances were disrupted by the fall of the Kanam Depa's principality in the late 1920s, the absorption of Po-yul by the Ganden Potrang state, and attempts by its local representatives to enforce tax collection in Pemako and beyond in the following decades. The McMahon line was of course drawn well south of the Tsangpo gorge in recognition of Tibetan claims to Pemako (tenuous though these were), but armed tax collection missions south of the line eventually prompted the British government of Assam to mount a task force to police the area (1943).[11] Only after independence, a permanent, administrative presence was established on the Indian side. The

McMahon line is nonetheless disputed in this sector since it included the southernmost reach of Tibetan Pemako (the village of Tuting and the Yangsang/Nyigong tributary valley), in Indian territory.

In lower Dzayul, or the upper Lohit valley, also an issue in the 1962 conflict, the position was similar. This was traditionally Deng territory that had been colonized by Tibetan migrants perhaps no earlier than the 19th century, and claimed by the Lhasa government in due course. This claim too was acknowledged by the McMahon line, which followed the customary border downstream of the village of Riga, and there are no historic Tibetan claims beyond that point.[12]

Finally, any assessment of China's claim to Arunachal has to ask why, if this is really seen as China's territory by the CCP leadership, did the troops withdraw, even from Tawang, in 1962?

Indian negotiators in 1959-60 were confused and a little incredulous to find that their Chinese counterparts offered no detailed argumentation or substantiation for their claim to the entire NEFA. For the Maoist regime, history was bunk, and the notion of objective truth was a bourgeois fiction. The Maoist state used lies, the bigger the better, frequently and loudly repeated, to bludgeon and numb its opponents. In the Maoist view, it is power, not intellectual or moral superiority, which wins arguments in the real world. Their historical claims to Tibet are of a similar nature.

Peking's main concern in the region at the time was consolidating control over Tibet in the aftermath of the 1959 uprising and subsequent Red Terror in which hundreds of thousands of Tibetans were killed or imprisoned in Gulags. China was still very insecure internationally at the time, and anticipated unfavourable reaction to its occupation and repression of a neighbouring country. Since Tibet was of no strategic interest to the "imperialist" powers by that time, India posed the main potential threat to international acquiescence, a threat confirmed by its willingness to grant asylum to the Dalai Lama and the flood of refugees who followed him into exile. India's docile and premature acquiescence in the occupation in the early 1950s now seemed less assured.

Rather than be caught on the defensive over its occupation of Tibet, the Maoist strategy was to attack, to claim more territory, a large enough piece of territory to grab attention, that China had never owned and had no serious intention of occupying. This strategy altered the terrain of Sino-Indian border diplomacy and confrontation in China's favour, away from Tibet (a core interest) and onto the jungles of NEFA (a marginal interest at best).

In the little Tawang enclave, they saw the potential for a territorial claim (India had after all disavowed the government with which it reached the 1914 agreement), and simply extrapolated this potential to the entire state (on the basis that it had not come under firm administration by Indian governments hitherto, and perhaps the idea that if a part of the McMahon line was invalid, it was invalid in its entirety).

In my submission, the border dispute is thus not really about the rightful ownership of Arunachal at all. It is about tying India down while China gets on with thoroughly subjugating and exploiting Tibet, and providing China with another foil in its bid for hegemony in South Asia.

Any meaningful discussion of the border with the Peoples Republic of China must therefore take into account India's legitimate interests in Tibet, the will of the Tibetan people, and of their Himalayan neighbours.

NOTES AND REFERENCES

1. The 'eastern Dung' mentioned in Tibetan sources appear to have been powerful rulers, and patrons of Tibetan Lamas, based in the lower regions of what is now known as Monyul. Two mid-15th century Tibetan works, the rGya bod yig tshang by Trehor Paljor Sangpo (Sichuan: Peoples Publishing House, 1985) p.291 and Jigme Drakpa's Dad pa'i lo thog dngos grub kyi char 'bebs biography of Rabten Kunsang Pakpa (Tibet Peoples Publishing House, 1987, pp.7-8), record military campaigns against them by the Sharkapa rulers of Gyantse in the mid-14th century, when they controlled southern districts of Tibet including Pari (Phag ri) and Lhodrak (lHo brag).
2. The founding legends and lineages of the kings of Monyul appear in rJe 'bangs rnams kyi rigs rus gsal ba'i sgron me (Mon chos byung) in "Selected materials on Tibetan culture and history" vol.10, produced by the History and culture materials research committee of the TAR branch of the Chinese Peoples Political Consultative Conference, Lhasa, 1988.
3. See e.g., Du ku la'i gos bzang vol.1, p.274; Mi dbang rtogs brjod p.160; Bod kyi srid don rgyal rabs vol. 1, pp. 431, 443).
4. Among the few literary testaments to these events is an unpublished history of the Geluk school in Monyul based on local sources titled Mon phyogs 'dzin ma'i char zhva ser gyi ring lugs di Itar dar ba'i lo rgyus dga' ba'i dpal ster ma, by one Khrom steng dge slong (cited by Aris, 1980).
5. Tubten Chopel, who was serving as abbot of Tawang in 1950, summarised the arrangement in an article intended to support China's claim to Tawang (The facts about India's military occupation of Monyul in Selected materials on Tibetan culture and history vol.10 1988): 'Following the Dalai Lama's instructions to Merak Lama and the Tsona Dingpon Namka Drukdrak, once administrative control of Monyul was established, the 'Tawang Shi-drel' (four joint officials) became the core of the administration: these were the one monastic and one lay official appointed by the Tibetan government to the Tawang Nyertsang

(monastery administration), and the abbot (Khenpo) and monastic administrator (Lama Lene) appointed by Loseling college. They were in charge of administration in the whole of Monyul. The 'Tawang Drukdrel' (six joint officials) meant the above four plus the one monastic and one lay official appointed to Tsona Dzong by the Tibetan government. When these officials received orders from the government, they passed them down to the four Dzongs under their administration—Sengge Dzong, Dirang Dzong, Taklung Dzong and Gyangkhar Dzong—and to the heads of the local communities, and they had full powers, such as adjudicating disputes and so on.

The 'Tawang Dundrel' (seven joint officials) meant the above six plus the Tsona rice procurement officer appointed by the (Tibetan government's) ecclesiastical bursary (Bla phyag las khung), who met to deal with issues concerning the transport of commodities, or any other specific issues that arose.

The 'Tawang Gu-drel' (nine joint officials) meant meetings of the 'Drukdrel' plus the headmen of the three Tso on the sunny side of the valley, called in response to important events. The chief of Mon Gyangkhar Dzong was appointed by Tsona Dzong and had concurrent authority over Sengge Dzong. The chiefs of Dirang Dzong and Taklung Dzong were appointed by the monastery general assembly from among its own monastic officials. The chief-elders of the three Tso (communities) on the sunny side of the valley had to register their names with the 'Shi-drel' or 'Drukdrel' offices for approval, and otherwise the chiefs of the Tso and Ding (smaller communities) were appointed after registering with the Drukdrel's tax collectors or the officials of the four Dzongs…' Compare this with Lieutenant-Colonel Bailey's account, who arrived in Tawang in October 1913 in the course of an informal survey that guided delineation of the McMahon Line: 'Monyul was governed by the Trukdri, a Council of Six, situated in Tawang. There was the Kenpo, or abbot, of Tawang, another high Lama, two monks known as Nyetsangs...and the two Dzongpons of Tsona or their agents. In the summer, when the heat was oppressive in Tawang, the Dzongpons went up to Tsona, leaving their agents to represent them in Tawang; and in the winter, when the cold was oppressive in Tsona, the Dzongpons came down to Tawang...' Bailey, a political officer with long and distinguished experience in the Himalaya and Tibet, leaves no doubt as to the efficacy of Tibetan administration in Tawang, F.M. Bailey, *Wo Passport to Tibet*, London, 1956, pp. 239-40.

6. N Lego, *Modern History of Arunachal Pradesh (1825-2006)*, Mrs Ponung Lego, Itanagar 2006 pp.6-10. This 2006 textbook, which states in its first few pages that Monyul belonged to Tibet, was approved for use in government schools in the state.
7. Report of the officials of the governments of India and the Peoples Republic of China on the boundary question, Ministry of External Affairs 1961. The relevant passages are found on pp. 121-28, pp. 219-24.
8. This is by no means a new position on the question: the arguments made in the Report of the officials were challenged at some length in volume 2 of Alastair Lamb's McMahon Line (1966).
9. Robert Barnett, "Did Britain Just Sell Tibet?", *New York Times*, November 24, 2008 accessed at http://www.nytimes.com/2008/11/25/opinion/25barnett.html?_r=0, accessed on June 14, 2013, also see Steve Tang (http://articles.timesofindia.indiatimes.com/2010-01-09/india/28139275_1), accessed on June 14, 2013.
10. See e.g., The Tibet local government did not go along with the exchange of secret letters in New Delhi by Lhalu Tsewang Dorje, and Encountering Indian invaders, I yelled at them by Markong Yeshe Dramdul, in "Selected materials on Tibetan culture and history" vol.10 Lhasa 1988 publisher. As in Tawang, the residual rights of Tibetan estate holders in

Pachakshri were taken into account by the 1914 agreement.

11. Toni Huber, "Pushing South: Tibetan economic and political activities in the far eastern Himalaya 1900-1950", in Buddhist Himalaya: studies in religion, history and culture, Golden Jubilee Conference, Namgyal Institute of Tibetology vol.1, Gangtok, 2008.
12. Ronald Kaulback, "The Assam border of Tibet", *The Geographical Journal*, vol.83, no.3, 1934. The historical background is touched on in The McMahon Line vol.2 p.318-19. The claim to a boundary downriver from Walong is a Chinese claim, rather than a Tibetan one, based on the furthest point reached by Qing expeditionary forces during the reconquest mission of 1910-12 (Vol.2, pp.540-45).

Chapter 10

Chinese Support to Northeast Indian Separatist Movements

Subir Bhaumik

The Chinese support for separatist movements in India's northeast should be seen as part of the larger post-colonial South Asian trend of hostile nation-states mutually backing insurgencies against each other. China and Myanmar, though not located in South Asia, are important players in the region. This phenomenon of mutual and reciprocal patronage to insurgencies in post-colonial South Asia has been examined, studied and argued in detail in my work, *Insurgent Crossfire (*1995), wherein I have established the reciprocity of patronage to insurgencies against hostile nation-states by most post-colonial South Asian nations.[1]

If Pakistan supported insurgencies in Kashmir and India's Northeast and later in Indian Punjab, India also backed the Bengali insurrection in 1971 to break up Pakistan and later backed separatist movements in Sindh and Baluchistan. If India backed the Shanti Bahini rebels of Chittagong Hill Tracts against Bangladesh, Dhaka also backed a whole range of Northeast Indian rebel groups until Sheikh Hasina came to power in 2009 and ordered a comprehensive crackdown on them to push them out and work towards a new era of friendship with India.

If India with the US backed the Tibetan insurrection in the 1950-60s and continued to support the Tibetan government in exile much to the chagrin of Beijing, China also backed a whole range of Northeast Indian insurgencies since the first batch of Naga rebels went to Yunnan for training in 1966. Only tiny Sri Lanka has not backed an insurgency on Indian soil in response to Indian backing for the LTTE and other Tamil rebel groups in Jaffna peninsula and Myanmar, which like China is a player in South Asia due to its proximity to the region, has not directly backed any rebel group against India, despite complaints that it has not firmly acted against a whole host of northeast Indian rebel groups based in its Sagaing division (euphemistically called "Eastern Nagaland").[2]

China, however, began to aid and abet the northeast Indian insurgencies only after the 1962 border war. Throughout the 1950s and early 1960s, when India with the help of US backed the violent insurrections in Tibet and trained a whole lot of Tibetan fighters in its training facilities across the Himalayas, China responded by warning India against backing "Tibetan counter-revolutionaries as part of imperialist designs".[3] Beijing's emphasis was on trying to get India out of the US Cold War game plans and work towards a resolution of the border dispute based on a swap—during Prime Minister Zhou En Lai's Delhi visit, China offered to accept India's position on the McMahon line if India recognized its position in the Aksai Chin-Ladakh sector. It is only after the 1962 Himalayan border war, that China decided to play into the pattern of "Insurgent crossfire"—rather than escalating another conventional war with India. Beijing decided to back rebel groups from India's northeast. It began with the support for the Naga National Army, several of whose batches were trained in China. The first batch went to Yunnan in the second part of 1966, led by Brigadier Thinoselie and Thuingaleng Muivah. The last batch of Naga rebels went to China for training and weapons in 1973.

China's patronage for northeastern Indian rebels thus began during the Great Proletarian Cultural Revolution, when the Chinese Communist Party was in a mood to "export revolution" like the Soviet Communists after the Great Bolshevik Revolution in 1917.

But though the first phase of Chinese patronage for northeast Indian rebels coincided with the beginning and the end of the Cultural Revolution, the predominantly Christian rebels from Naga and Mizo tribes were hardly subjected to any "Communist indoctrination". Only Thuingaleng Muivah was extensively exposed to the political ideology of Marxism-Leninism and Mao Tse-tung's thought because he already had an exposure to Leftist ideology.[4]

On the contrary, the small batch of rebels from Manipur's People's Liberation Army (formed in 1976) that went to China for training in the late 1970s were extensively indoctrinated in Marxism-Leninism and Mao's thought. They were not even given weapons but were asked to come back to Manipur and build a revolutionary peoples guerilla army by snatching weapons from Indian security forces.[5] Later, as the PLA expanded into a powerful urban guerilla force capable of also fighting jungle guerrilla war, they began to covertly import Chinese weapons but from black market sources in Southeast Asia. But, with the end of the Cultural Revolution, the demise of Mao Tse-tung and the rise of Teng Hsiao-ping, the Chinese government backed off from supporting the Northeast Indian insurgent groups. The long journeys that the rebels made to Yunnan through Burma's Kachin Hills stopped and the northeast Indian rebel groups also had difficulty in maintaining any presence in the Kachin state because of the leading anti-Yangon rebel group, Kachin Independence Organisation (KIO), developed close relations with Indian intelligence and asked the northeastern groups to clear off from their base area. The access to the Kachin corridor is vital for northeast Indian rebel groups wanting to make to China's Yunnan province in large groups on foot.

India also started to engage China, first in the Janata government's time when foreign minister A B Vajpayee visited Beijing, and then when the Congress was back in power. Prime Minister Rajeev Gandhi's visit laid the foundation for improved relations after the two countries had nearly come to war after reported Chinese incursions in Sumdorong Chu (Tawang-Bumla sector) in 1986-87. The Treaty of Peace and Tranquility that the two countries signed in 1993 stabilised relations between the two Asian giants and led to demilitarization of the Himalayan frontier. But, though Chinese support for northeast Indian rebel groups (and even the Burmese ethnic and communist rebels) stopped, Chinese intelligence did maintain links with the likes of NSCN leader Muivah.

In recent years, however, intelligence and media reports have began to surface about renewed contacts between Chinese intelligence and northeastern rebel groups. The immediate provocation for such a step was India developing a "strategic relationship" with the US on the back of the Indo-US nuclear deal. Senior Chinese diplomats have told this writer that, much as they realized India's need for energy as a fast growing economy like China itself, they were peeved at the "strategic relationship" with US. One Chinese diplomat in India said this was aimed at "strategic encirclement "of China that is part of the US game plan and that he said could manifest in (a) closer military ties between India, Australia, US, Japan and other Asian neighbours of China (b) reopening a covert front in Tibet by India and the US (c) greater number of military exercises by India and the US along with the militaries of other Asian countries that had sent a feel-threatened signal to China.[6]

So, China could well be using renewed contact with northeast Indian rebel groups as a way to deter and counter-pressure India into dropping out of the US plans to "encircle" China. But this would be one of the many manifestations of China's counter-strategy to stymie Indo-US plans. The other Chinese hostile measures include reopening the border question by claiming Arunachal Pradesh as "southern Tibet" and aggressively cultivating Delhi's neighbours to set up military bases all around India as part of a "counter-encirclement" strategy.

There has been some stray reports of ULFA leaders meeting Chinese intelligence officials since the beginning of 2008, but they were never confirmed. Now, confirmation has been received of two meetings that ULFA Commander in Chief Paresh Barua, Manipur PLA chairman Irengbam Bhorot and All Tripura Tiger Force chairman Ranjit Debbarma had with senior Chinese military intelligence officials this year.[7] Following this meeting, atleast three batches of guerilla fighters of ULFA and PLA left for locations on Sino-Myanmar border for training. Paresh Barua, ULFA C-in-C, first flew to Kumming in Yunnan province from Dhaka and had two meetings with Chinese Military intelligence officials between 13-17 February, 2009. Then he flew to Beijing from Bangkok on 23rd May 2009 and was in the Chinese capital for four days. On both occasions, he was received by one Colonel of the Second Department of the Chinese Peoples Liberation Army General Staff of Military Intelligence Directorate who introduced himself as Xiu Rongji (could well be a pseudonym). During his trip to Beijing, Barua was taken to the "Second Department" head office, which is located at No. 21, North Andeli Street, Beijing, The place is heavily guarded but has no signboards.

Barua was accompanied by Irengbam Bhorot, chairman of PLA (Manipur). The chief of Chinese Military Intelligence Department, one Lieutenant General Guangkhai gave them audience on two occasions. The Chinese general encouraged the Northeastern rebel leaders to regroup and step up recruitment and not be weighed down by current losses and setbacks; he also promised to train new recruits and provide latest weaponry. He told the Northeastern rebel leaders that India will never do justice to the smaller nationalities because they were never Indians but were colonised by the British and handed over to India after 1947. He also denounced India as an "US lackey" and said it is no longer an independent country.

General Guangkhai's argument sounds similar to the one in the controversial article of the website www.chinaiiss.org, which is the website of the Institute for International Strategic Studies, the research wing of the Second Department. This research institute is no independent think tank but its job is to produce for military intelligence an internal classified publication "Movements of Foreign Armies" [WAI JUN DONGTAI]. This is published in every 10 days and transmitted to units at the division level.

Following the parleys between the Northeastern rebel leaders, a total of 78 ULFA and PLA rebels left for the Sino-Myanmar border in three batches in June 2009. These batches have completed their training and now set up consolidated bases at Taga in the the Hukawng valley, an area dominated by NSCN's Khaplang faction. These three batches were trained by instructors of the Chinese army who belong to the Lisu tribe. Leaders like Paresh Barua knew who they were but they were introduced as Kachin instructors to the northeast Indian rebel recruits.

It is anybody's guess what kind of training these rebels are receiving from China but general intelligence assessment suggests they would receive extensive training in (a) guerrilla warfare, (b) explosives, (c) espionage, (d) select assassination, and (e) computer and electronics communication. Though, these rebels will primarily operate against Indian security forces in the Northeast, some of them may be used by the Chinese to attack important Tibetan exile leaders in Indian territory. They may do this in coordination with already infiltrated Chinese agents operating in India.

But this whole effort was part of the massive regrouping exercise of the northeast Indian rebel groups in the Upper Myanmar region after they were forced to leave Bangladesh. Now, the best fighters of the ULFA, PLA (Manipur), NSCN (Khaplang) and several other groups have been conducting training of new batches of rebels who have made their way to the Hukawng valley to join the separatist movements. Altogether 14 northeast Indian rebel groups have set up bases around Taga and have set up an united front, right at a time when Rajeev Bhattacharyya, executive editor of the Seven Sisters Post that I edit, was present there.[8] Some of these groups have only a token presence there and sent their cadres for training and some leaders are left behind to liaise with the major groups, who have big camps and house hundred of fighters who stay safe out of the operational range of the Indian army and can make their way back for special missions and attacks.

The importance of the Hukawng valley zone for the northeast Indian rebels is considerable. If this base area is attacked and demolished by Myanmar army, *a la* Bhutan 2003, the rebels from India's northeast will lose their last major trans-border base area and their ability to procure weapons, train new recruits and keep leaders and core fighters groups beyond the operational reach of the Indian forces will become drastically limited. These rebels, will also loose their land access to China. In future, if relations between China and India worsen, China may step up assistance more directly to these rebel groups and seek to use them as "force multipliers" both in direct conventional war or in "proxy war" situations. India may have to deal with these rebels as agent provocateurs out to thwart the country's defence effort in the event of a Chinese military offensive.

NOTES AND REFERENCES

1. Subir Bhaumik, *Insurgent Crossfire*, Hurst (UK), 1995 and Lancers (Delhi), 1996
2. Detailed reports of Rajeev Bhattacharyya in Assam-based English daily, *Seven Sisters Post*, Feb 2-14, 2012. Bhattacharyya trekked hundreds of kilometers in "Eastern Nagaland" and enjoyed rare access to all the Northeastern rebel groups and even witnessed the coming together of a united front of 14 such groups during his stay in the area between November 2011 and January 2012.
3. Karki Hussain, *Sino Indian Conflict and International Politics in the Indian Sub-Continent, 1962-66*, Thomson Press, Delhi, 1977.
4. Thuingaleng Muivah, "Never Say Die," interview by author, Mannerplaw, Thailand, published in Sunday magazine, Kolkata, June 16-22, 1996.
5. Subir Bhaumik, *Troubled Periphery: Crisis of India's Northeast*, Sage, New Delhi, 2009.
6. Mao Siwei, Chinese consul-general in Calcutta, interview with author, 8th November 2009.
7. Subir Bhaumik's blog in **www.bengalnewz.com**, "China starts backing India's north-east rebels", 11th September 2009
8. Details of the training of the northeastern rebels and the creation of the united front that brings together 14 rebel groups are available in Rajeev Bhattacharyya's reports in *Seven Sisters Post* between 2nd and 14th February 2012.

Chapter 11

Resolving Sino-Indian Border Dispute: Overcoming Nationalist Myopia

H. Srikanth

Introduction

Most border disputes that post-colonial states have experienced have their roots in the omissions and commissions of colonial rule.[1] The urge to expand and protect the frontiers of the empires forced the colonial rulers to draw and redraw the boundaries of their colonies. At times, the fear of expansion by the enemy forces forced the colonial powers to create buffer zones. Taking advantage of the weakness of the native rulers, the colonial powers often compelled the neighboring countries to accept the border proposals, which are not to their interest and liking. Linear demarcations of the borders by the colonizers overlooked the traditional boundaries of the native communities and kingdoms. The concerns of the people inhabiting the border areas were never in their minds while preparing boundary maps. Naturally, the people were never consulted while drawing the borders. The decisions as to what should be the borders were taken by officials who hardly represented the peoples. The project of anti-colonial national liberation struggles should have exposed the colonial interests and manipulations, and united the decolonized people to think afresh about their boundaries, without letting the colonial baggage dictate their minds and actions. But unfortunately, even after decolonization, the lines marked as borders by the colonial powers in their colonial interest are fueling border disputes among the post-colonial nation states, affecting the friendly relations between the people on either side of the borders. The unfortunate war of 1962 and the unresolved border dispute between India and China point out the continuing hold of colonization on the minds of politically decolonized people.

Limits of Nationalist Perceptions

Historically, nationalism is a progressive force as long as it is fighting against feudalism and colonialism. But once nation state becomes a reality, nationalism can become a tool in the hands of reactionaries for misleading and manipulating the citizens of a nation state for serving the interests of certain privileged classes or groups of people.[2] If one is only a nationalist, he or she can never see the mistakes and limitations of his or her own nation and blindly support whatever the ruling elite think and do in the name of nation. This is true of both capitalist and socialist nations. If citizens are blinded by national jingoism and chauvinism, even fellow travelers appear as enemies. In the world of nation states where we live in, becoming a true internationalist may not be an easy task. But at least one should learn to take a critical look at what all is advocated or justified in the name of nation and national interests. Unless one learns to interrogate nationalism itself, it will never be possible for one to understand the stand of other nations whom are viewed as enemies or competitors.

In India, the elite consensus and the effective media management have made the citizens believe that India has been an innocent victim of the Chinese aggression in 1962 and that China has been in possession of thousands of square miles or kilometers of territory that legitimately belong to India. So much has been said and written along these lines by politicians, military officials, and journalists and scholars in India.[3] Many intellectuals in the universities and the research organizations in India passively and selectively quote these and some other foreign sources to make case in defense of India, or against China. But very few dare to interrogate the basis on which India's territorial claims against China rest. What they believe to be Sino-Indian borders are not borders drawn by Indians in consultation with its neighbors. These are the borders conceived and proposed by the British colonizers in their own colonial interest. There was no Indian representative in any of the talks or discussions that took place between British India, Tibet and China. Why is it that Indians who fought against the British colonial rule and achieved independence then started to consider the borders drawn by British colonial rulers as sacrosanct?[4] It is a well-known fact that China never ratified the Simla Agreement of 1914, wherein an attempt was made to incorporate McMahon Line as the border between Tibet and India without the knowledge of China.[5] Since India, like many other states in the world, recognizes Tibet as an integral part of China, how can McMahon Line become the border between India and China, unless China also agrees to it? The same is the case in the western sector, wherein India is claiming Aksai Chin area based on Johnson's map, or some imaginary historical evidences that have no place in international law. The argument that India has been in possession of this territory from the time immemorial[6] holds no ground, for India as a nation state is of recent origin. Of course, as a civilizational entity, India did exist for centuries. But the 'cultural borders' of Indian civilization need not coincide with the borders of Indian nation state. If Aksai Chin and Thagla Ridge areas are claimed as part of the Indian Territory based only on what the Hindu scriptures have said,[7] then India should also claim many other areas in Pakistan and Afghanistan as well. By that logic India should also give up some of the territories in northeast India, which were never a part of the so-called Indian civilization. What the colonial rulers did or what the Hindu scriptures and folklore said cannot become rational bases for national territorial claims.

Perceptions and Truth

Through relentless nationalist and imperialist propaganda and because of legal or illegal ban on information that contradict the nationalist assumptions, common citizens of India believe that it was China that attacked India. But today the readers have access to writings of eminent scholars like Bertrand Russell, Neville Maxwell, Steven A Hoffman, Karunakar Gupta, A.G. Noorani etc., who showed that India's territorial claims are not full-proof and that the war became inevitable because of India's adventurist Forward Policy and its refusal to negotiate with China on borders.[8] Presenting China's version, Garver argued that the China's action was prompted by two sets of perceptions: First, the feeling that India was trying to undermine China's control over Tibet and second, that India needs to be punished for eyeing on the Chinese territory.[9] Without heeding China's protests, India went ahead creating posts north of McMahon Line, wrongly claiming that its boundaries extend up to Thagla Ridge. Books like *Himalayan Blunder: The Curtain Raiser to the Sino-Indian War of 1962* by Brig. J.P. Dalvi (Retd) and *The Guilty Men of 1962* by D.R. Mankekar tell us how the junior officials in the Ministry of Defence passed orders forcing the Indian Army to go ahead with setting up posts (such as Khinzamene and Dhola posts) north of McMahon Line, although the military officials operating on the ground were not in favor of it.[10] As such, India not only insisted that McMahon Line is its border with China, but also decided on its own which areas come within its purview. India refused to listen to China's repeated requests for negotiations and ignored its threats of retributions.[11] Based on the assumption that China would never go for a large-scale attack, Indian think-tank in Delhi decided to carry on its Forward policy coded Operation "Leghorn". Finally Nehru's much publicized comments at the Delhi airport on October 12, 1962, on his way to Colombo, wherein it was stated that the government has given orders to the Indian Army to evict the Chinese intruders from "our territory", made China believe that only through war it can teach a lesson to India.

The Chinese attack on India in 1962 gave an opportunity for India and the imperialist forces to project it as an act of aggression. But they had no convincing answers as to why the Chinese forces after advancing almost up to Tezpur, unilaterally declared ceasefire and withdrew its forces from the occupied areas.[12] Given that China never accepted McMahon Line as its boundary, what would have prevented it from retaining Tawang and other parts of Arunachal Pradesh that it had occupied, if it really had an eye on them? The manner in which the Chinese army behaved with the people of NEFA and the captured Indian army men, their limited interest seemed to be to push back the advancing Indian military which was setting up posts in the north of McMahon Line and to show to India that China should not be taken lightly. Reflecting on the events, Brig. Dalvi, whose nationalist credentials cannot be doubted, had remarked, "The Chinese in 1962 had prepared both for war and for talks, if India appreciated the futility of fighting for her rights. India was prepared neither for fighting nor for talking".[13] The records show that throughout this period, India's Forward policy was premised on the assumption that Chinese would not attack. But when the 'swift and massive retribution' started, it came as a shock even to man like General Kaul, who reportedly cried, "Oh my God! You are right, they mean business".[14]

War or Negotiations?

The experience of the 1962 War gives us an indication that war is a bad option for resolving the border dispute. It is true that since 1962, India has diverted much of its meager resources to build up its military strength. Indian military capabilities have substantially increased after 1962. But it also needs to be kept in mind that China is a strong military force in the world today. More worrying to India is the fact that China today has drifted from socialist ideals and has virtually become a capitalist power. The socialist leaders like Zhou-Enlai and Mao Zedong, who know when to start and stop the war, are no longer at the helm of affairs in China. Under the new regime, China which is practicing an out and out capitalist path of development in the name of socialist market economy, is whipping up national feelings to seek legitimacy.[15] Given the change in the class character of the China's political elite, to what extent China goes in the event of another war is something not predictable at this stage. On their part, the imperialist forces are ever ready to take advantage of the war, if it breaks again. Hence, if there is going to be another war between India and China, then that would be more brutal and devastating. In 1962, China ensured that the people of the region do not suffer in any manner. In the present context, irrespective of which nation ultimately wins or loses, the people of Arunachal Pradesh will be the first and the worst sufferers of the war. So, the most sensible alternative left for India is to engage China in a meaningful, rational and reasonable dialogue.

Here, it is necessary to remember that China has borders with 12 countries. Neville Maxwell who made a study of the China's border policy towards its neighbors shows that barring brief rift with Soviet Union and Vietnam, China negotiated borders with all other neighbors, on the basis of Chou-Enlai's border policy enunciated in the Bandung Conference of 1956.[16] Thus so far, in its negotiations with its neighbors, China never claimed suzerainty over all territories over which its pre-colonial rulers held a sway. It realizes the need for mutually beneficial negotiated settlement of all border disputes. Smaller nations like Pakistan, Nepal, Myanmar, Mongolia etc., have negotiated borders with China without much difficulty. Hence, there is no reason to think that China would be averse to meaningful dialogue with India, unless India becomes sufficiently powerful enough to enforce its will over China. However, negotiations would not move an inch forward, if India continues to stick to its pre-1962 position. Neither McMahon Line, nor Johnson's Map could be insisted as the bases for talks. It is humiliating for the proud people of both India and China which fought against colonialism and feudalism to base their negotiations on what the colonizers did in their own interest. Negotiations should consider history, geographical realities, present administrative, economic and other activities in the region and also religion, custom, language and such other features that generate deep-rooted sentiments and emotions. While presenting one's case, both the parties should be receptive to the arguments, sentiments and strategic concerns of the other. India is not the only country which has sentimental attachment to the Himalayas. India does not need to bring in McMahon to argue its case for Arunachal Pradesh. The very fact that since independence the people of Arunachal Pradesh have been part of India, voluntarily associated and identified themselves with the Indian Union and that their allegiance to India is demonstrated in their participation in national political processes are enough to argue that Arunachal Pradesh has become a part of India nation state. The exact alignments between Arunachal Pradesh and China can be decided after joint survey and consultations. Similarly, India needs to recognize the ground reality that Aksai Chin continues to be under the control of China and that geographically and economically the region makes little sense to India.[17] Earlier, China gave the hint that it would recognize McMahon in return for India giving up its claims over Aksai Chin. Scholars like John Lall, also feel that it is better option open for India.[18] Although, the political regime in China has changed, the Chinese authorities may still be favorable to the idea. If necessary, to placate the nationalist sentiments of the people of both the countries, some uninhabited parts of along eastern front can be given to China and in return China could reciprocate some territories to India in the western front. India, which had whipped up national sentiments on the issue of Aksai Chin may find it difficult to change its position, given the manner in which the parliamentary politics works. However, the task is not all that impossible. When India, unable to resolve Kashmir problem, is showing its willingness to give up 'Azad Kashmir' and accept the Line of Control as border between India and Pakistan, there is no reason why it cannot give up geographically inaccessible, economically unviable and sparsely populated Aksai Chin, in return for retaining Arunachal Pradesh with India. If India could achieve political consensus on this issue, there is likelihood of China giving up its claim over Arunachal Pradesh. The aspirations of the millions of people in Arunachal Pradesh are more important to India than securing control over the Soda plains of Aksai Chin.

Conclusion

Given everyday tensions along the borders, it is necessary for both India and China to resolve the border dispute as early as possible.[19] As long as the border dispute persists, the reactionary ruling elite would be using it to whip up national sentiments, create war psychosis, divert the scarce national resources to meet the defense needs and distract attention of the people from more significant domestic problems and crises. The people in both the countries should therefore realize that war is not in their interest. They should buildup strong pressure within their own countries forcing their governments to resolve border dispute by adopting rational and reasonable approach. The hawks in both the countries have to be restrained by encouraging people-to-people contact and by building up strong peace movement in both the countries. It is high time the people of India and China came out of the colonial baggage, gave up rigidities and looked at border problem from the view-point of what would be in the best and long-term interests of the people of both countries.

NOTES AND REFERENCES

1. Most territorial disputes in the world today are between post-colonial states. See, "List of Territorial Disputes", Wikipedia, accesssed at http://en.wikipedia.org/wiki/List_of_territorial_disputes accessed on March 13, 2012. That colonialism has been the root cause of border disputes is recognized in Asia, Africa and Latin America. Refer, Emmanuel N. Amadife, James W. Warhola, "Africa's Political Boundaries: Colonial Cartography, the OAU, and the Advisability of Ethno-National Adjustment", *International Journal of Politics, Culture, and Society*, 6 (Summer, 1993): 533-554; Gwenn Okruhlik, Patrick J. Conge, "The Politics of Border Disputes: On the Arabian Peninsula", *International Journal*, 54 (Spring, 1999): 230-248; Stephen A. Kocs, "Territorial Disputes and Interstate War, 1945-1987", *The Journal of Politics*, 57 (February, 1995):159-175; Adekunle Ajala, "The Nature of African Boundaries", *Africa Spectrum*, 18 (1983): 177-189; Alastair Lamb, *Asian Frontiers: Studies in a Continuing Problem*, Pall Mass Press, London, 1968.
2. V.I. Lenin, *The Right of Nations to Self Determination*: *Critical Remarks on the National Question and the Right of Nations to Self-Determination*, Progress Publishers, Moscow, 1971; Chris Harman, *The Return of the National Question*, International Socialism (Autumn 1992):3-61, accesed at http://www.marxists.org/archive/harman/1992/xx/natquest.htm#f12, accessed March 14, 2012.
3. V.B. Karnik ed., *China Invades India,* George Allen & Unwin, *London*, 1963; Lt. Gen. B.M. Kaul, *The Untold Story,* Allied Publishers, Bombay, 1967; P.B. Sinha, A.A. Athale, S.N. Prasad eds., *History of the Conflict with China, 1962*, History Division, Ministry of Defence, Government of India, New Delhi, 1992; J.S. Dalal, *The Sino-Indian Border Dispute: India's Current Options*, U.S. Army Command and General Staff College, Kansas, 1993; B.N. Mullick, *My Years with Nehru: The Chinese Betrayal,* Allied Publishers, Bombay, 1972.
4. Reacting to India's stand on borders, Arnold Toynbee observed, "It is queer that lines drawn by British officials should have been consecrated as precious national assets of the British Indian Empire's non-British successor states.... The present consecration of these British-made lines as heirlooms in the successor states' national heritages is an unexpected and

unfortunate turn of History's wheel." Another scholar, Alaistair Lamb, the author of the two volumes on McMahon Line wondered, "Why Mr. Nehru, while declaring himself committed to a policy of friendship, of peaceful co-existence, with Communist China, should have adhered with such tenacity to those symbols, at least in Chinese eyes, of British Imperialism, the Simla Convention and the McMahon Line notes, is one of the mysteries of the twentieth century." Both quoted in Suniti Kumar Ghosh, *The Himalayan Adventure: India-China War of 1962: Causes and Consequences*, Research Unit of Political Economy, Bombay, 2002 accessed at www.marxists.org/.../india/ghosh/2002/himalayan-adventure/index.htm, accessed March 14, 2012.

5. Scholars like Neville Maxwell and Karunakar Gupta have argued in several of their writings that China was not consulted on McMahon Line and that the objective of the Shimla Conference, 1914 was not to discuss McMahon Line. In one of his articles, Maxwell writes, "Sir Henry McMahon used the occasion (Simla Conference of 1914) to arrange secret bilateral negotiations in Delhi in March 1914 in which the Tibetan representative was induced to accept the desired new border line. .... That map was not shown, of course, to the Chinese representative at the conference. But McMahon tricked him into initialing a different map, on a very small scale, while purporting to illustrate only a proposed division of Tibet into Inner and Outer zones, also incorporated McMahon's secretly drawn alignment." See, Neville Maxwell, "Sino-Indian Border Dispute Reconsidered", *Economic and Political Weekly*, 34 (April 10, 1999): 907.

6. Till 1959 even Jawaharlal Nehru admitted that Aksai Chin was a disputed area. But it is said that Dr. S. Gopal, the then Director of the Historical Division of the Ministry of External Affairs, Government of India, convinced Nehru with 'historical arguments' in support of India's claims over Kashmir and Aksai Chin. Later other nationalist scholars also started using 'thousand years of Indian history' to justify India's claims. Much of these arguments are rubbished by scholars who held that they are not legally relevant. Refer, K. Krishna Rao, "The Sino-Indian Boundary Question and International Law", International and Comparative Law Quarterly, 11(1962): 375-384; Neville Maxwell, *India's China War,* Penguin Books, London, 1972, pp. 118-119; Karunakar Gupta, "Distortions in the History of Sino-Indian Frontiers", *Economic and Political Weekly*, 15, (July 26, 1980): 1270.

7. Addressing a public meeting in Agra on November 10, 1959, Nehru gave Hindu mythical twist to the border issue, by stating that the Himalayas were the essence of India's life and thought for ages. Commenting on the event Taya Zinkin, "The Prime Minister's speech at Agra was significant not for what he said but for the way he said it. For the first time since the Chinese started their pinprick machinegun technique on Ladakh border, he spoke as a Hindu. He told his audience that the Himalayas were India's 'Crown' and he referred to the sacred nature of these mountains which were woven into Indian thought, as part of the life blood of Hinduism" Quoted in Gupta, ibid.

8. Some other works of the scholars other than those mentioned thus far include, Karunakar Gupta, *The Hidden History of the Sino-Indian Frontier*, Minerva Associates Publications, Kolkata, 1974, 176p; Bertrand Russell, *Unarmed Victory*, Simon and Schuster, New York, 1963, 155p.; A.G. Noorani, "India's Forward Policy", *China Quarter*ly, vol-43 (July-September, 1970): 136-141; A.G. Noorani, *India China Boundary Problem, 1846-1947: History and Diplomacy,* OUP, New Dehi, 2011.

9. Officially India accepted Tibet as autonomous part of China and discouraged any discussion on it in the United Nations. Yet the asylum given to Dalai Lama and official or unofficial encouragement given to the Tibetan rebels during the fifties made China feel that India was trying to weaken China's control over China. For more details on Chinese perceptions

on India's role in Tibet, refer John W. Garver, "China's Decision for War with India in 1962", 2010, p. 2; accessed at http://chinaindiaborderdispute.files.wordpress.com/2010/07/garver.pdf, accessed on March 12, 2012.

10. Army and Assam Rifles officers on the ground, like Brig. J.P. Dalvi, General Umrao Singh, Major General Niranjan Prasad warned against setting up posts north of McMahon Line. But Delhi imposed the decision on the reluctant officers. Questioning who actually instructed them to create Dhola Post. Brig. J. P. Dalvi writes, "the Thagla-Dhola area was not strictly territory that "we should have been convinced was ourts"... and someone is guilty of exceeding the limits prescribed by him" Refer, Brig. J.P. Dalvi (Retd), *Himalayan Blunder: The Curtain Raiser to the Sino-Indian War of 1962,* Natraj Publishers, Dehra Dun, 2010 edn., p.136; For other details on the Dhola controversy, see also, D.R. Mankekar, *The Guilty Men of 1962,* The Tulshi Shah Enterprises, Bombay, 1968.

11. For China's official position on the 1962 War, refer, Government of People's Republic of China, "The Sino-Indian Boundary Question, Statement of the Government of People's Republic of China", Foreign Languages Press, Peking, 1962, accessed at http://www.marxists.org/subject/india/sino-india-boundary-question/ch01.htm; accessed on June 14, 2013, also see Garver, China's Decision for War with India in 1962.

12. Appreciating China's voluntary ceasefire and withdrawal of forces, Bertrand Russell, author of the book, *Unarmed Victory,* who tried to negotiate between India and China during the war period, wrote, "I cannot think of any other instance in which a victorious army has been halted in this way by its own Government." Quoted in Ghosh, *Himalayan Adventure.*

13. Dalvi, Himalayan Blunder, 149.

14. Quoted in Noorani, "India's Forward Policy".

15. That People's Republic of China is no more a socialist state is an established fact. See, Susan Williams, *Capitalism's Brutal Comeback in China,* Red Letter Press, Seattle, 2003; Andy McInerney, *China: Revolution and Counterrevolution,* PSL Publications, San Francisco, 2008; Lance Gore, *The Chinese Communist Party and China's Capitalist Revolution: The Political Impact of Market,* Routledge, New York, 2011; Guoguang Wu, Helen Lansdowne eds., *Socialist China, Capitalist China: Social Tension and Political Adaptation Under Economic Globalization,* Routledge, New York, 2009; Christopher Hughes, *Chinese Nationalism in the Global Era,* Routledge, New York, 2006.

16. For China's border policy, refer, Neville Maxwell, "Settlements and Disputes: China's Approach to Territorial Issues", *Economic and Political Weekly,* 41 (September 9, 2006): 3876-78; Nie Hongyi, "Explaining Chinese Solutions to Territorial Disputes with Neighboring States", *Chinese Journal of International Politics,* 2 (2009): 487-523.

17. Even General Thimaiah and Foreign Secretary, Mr. Dutt held that Aksai Chin was strategically not important and logically not maintainable. To quote him, "Even if the Chinese did not encroach into it, India could not make any use of it. The boundary had not been demarcated and had been shifted more than once by the British. There was an old silk route [across it] which ... the Chinese had only improved to make their road. It would be pointless to pick quarrels over issues in which India had no means of enforcing her claims." (Quoted in Maxwell, "Sino-Indian Border Dispute Reconsidered", 910). See also, Steven A Hoffman, *India and the China Crisis,* University of California Press, Berkeley, 1990, pp. 76-77. Much later, in his Convocation Address in JNU, Mr. K.P.S. Menon, the first Foreign Secretary openly stated that "it cannot be forgotten that Aksai Chin is of no importance to India, whereas, to China, it is of utmost importance, because it is the link between two historically troublesome regions, Tibet and Sinkiang." Quoted in Ghosh, *Himalayan Adventure.*

18. John Lall, *Aksai Chin and Sino-Indian Conflict,* Allied Publishers Ltd, New Delhi, 1989.
19. "Demarkation of Sino-Indian Border an Urgent Necessity", Proletarian Era, 43 (March 1, 2009) accessed at http://www.suci-c.in/download2009/pe03012009.pdf accessed on June 14, 2013.

Chapter 12

Can India and China Rekindle Bhai-Bhai Spirit in the 21st Century?

Jajati K Pattnaik

The 21st century is being touted as an Asian century. India and China, having civilisational linkages and enormous capabilities, are all set to steer the destiny of Asia and the world as the locus of global power configuration is being drifted from the West to the East. But, this Asian reawakening can only be sustained if these two Asian giants rekindle their much talked about bhai-bhai spirit and prioritise their interests and foreign policy objectives in the changing global context based on mutual trust and interdependence. Much to the chagrin of New Delhi, the recent assertions of Beijing over Arunachal Pradesh have evoked strong responses from the Indian side. Nevertheless, it goes to the credit of the leaderships of the two countries that in spite of all these, India and China have stayed engaged with each other and are enhancing interactions at various levels to sustain the pace of bilateral relationship. Taking due cognizance of the historical turns and twists in Sino-Indian relations, this chapter analyses various issues pertaining to India-China relations in contemporary perspective and conclude with several observations during the course of the discussion to strengthen their bilateral relations in future.

Backdrop of India-China Relations

To begin with, foreign policy is a set of principles pursued by the sovereign nation states to achieve national interest during the course of its relations at the bilateral as well as multilateral levels. The avowed realists describe national interest in the idiom of power looked from the perspective of material or military capability. On the contrary, the idealists interpret national interest in the language of universal moral principles and world peace.[1] The theoretical underpinnings of Indian foreign policy evolved during the cold war era were neither based on pure idealism nor realism but they were thrust upon 'enlightened self-interest' to match the divergent interests of nations.[2] India signed *Panchsheel* agreement with China on 29 April 1954, enunciating five principles such as: (i) mutual respect for each other's territorial integrity and sovereignty; (ii) mutual non-aggression; (iii) mutual non-interference; (iv) equality and mutual benefit; and (v) peaceful co-existence to promote international co-operation.[3] While defending *Panchsheel* Nehru said:

> It is no spirit of pride or arrogance that we pursue our independent policy. We would not do otherwise unless we are false to everything India has stood for in the past and stands for today. We welcome association and friendship with all and the flow of thought and ideas of all kind, but we reserve the right to choose our path. That is the essence of Panchsheel.[4]

However, India-China border conflict in 1962 proved as a great impediment in their bilateral relations. The entire gamut of bilateral relations was put in the cold storage. Finally, the ice was broken by the former Prime Minister Rajiv Gandhi when he showed goodwill gesture paying visit to Beijing in 1988.[5] With the collapse of Soviet Union in 1989, the cold war politics came to an end. The neo-liberal paradigm was propped up to facilitate free movement of trade, capital, knowledge, technology and labour across the globe. India ushered economic reforms in the nineties to deal with the emerging trends of globalisation.[6] The sustained growth rate during this period brought India's global economic influence, which led to projections that India would succeed many European countries as well as Japan by 2020 and United States by 2050.[7] The economic breakthrough redeemed India's position as major power in global politics. Correspondingly, China brought in guided neo-liberal reforms and emerged as the fastest growing economy in the world. The rise of India and China was duly acknowledged by the global powers. The foreign policy watchers perceived the swinging of power structure from the West to the East. Even the US Intelligence Council Report on Mapping Global Future informed that 'International community will have to confront the military, political and economic dimensions of the rise of China and India. It likened the emergence of China and India in the early twenty first century to the rise of Germany in the nineteenth century and America in the twentieth century with impacts potentially as dramatic'.[8] Notwithstanding the merits of such perceptions, the logic of those arguments lies on how far India and China translate them into action in building bridges for vibrant relations.

Revisiting the Past and Realising the Potentialities

India and China can shape the contours of contemporary international relations revisiting their glorious past and realising their immense potentialities. The soft power configurations and rich cultural past, demographic dividends, prosperous diaspora, geo-strategic locations and sustainable economic growth models have become significant variables to determine their bilateral as well as multilateral relations. In this context, India and China can set the stage through their soft power resources which are more pronounced to them compared to their global counterparts. The Harvard scholar, Joseph Nye, defines soft power as "the ability to get what you want through attraction rather than through coercion" as contrast to hard power which is based on "military force, coercion and intimidation".[9] Further, Nye says: "the soft power of a country rests primarily on three resources: its culture (in places where it is attractive to others), its political values (when it lives up to them at home and abroad), and its foreign policies (when they are seen as legitimate and having moral authority)".[10] So, the definitional interpretation of soft power indicates in drawing the resources of a nation from culture, domestic institutions, values, and art of diplomacy or foreign policy behaviour. Nye does not confine his views to the intangible resources of the US only, but he perceived for many nations attaining such derivatives in future. He observed that the ICT (Information and Communication Technology) environment would ease the process of gaining soft power status for: "those whose dominant cultures and ideals are closer to prevailing global norms (which now emphasize liberalism, pluralism, autonomy); those with the most access to multiple channels of communication and thus exercise more influence over how issues are framed; and those whose credibility is enhanced by their domestic and international performance".[11]

Indian soft power is sustained on civilizational ethos, democratic governance and diverse cultural mosaic displayed in art, literature, dance, music, song, cuisine and meditation (Yoga). India is the land of world's two great religions. Hinduism and Buddhism originated in India and later spread to South and South East Asia. These religio-philosophies brought in 'Hindu-Buddhist cosmological structure' and China 'absorbed it within its Confucian international order'.[12] The Indian film industry (Bollywood), cricket IPL

(Indian Premier League), Indian music, Yoga as well as Ayurveda have got a global niche and remained the sources of attraction for other nations. On the other, the Chinese soft power is based on cultural traditions, language, literature, philosophy, medicine, art and architecture, cuisine and martial art (Wushu) or (Kung Fu). Indian Yoga and Chinese Wushu or Kung Fu has really done wonders drawing attention across the globe. China is also using tools of cultural diplomacy to obtain universal approval propagating values of harmonious living and peaceful ascendance establishing Confucius Centres abroad, announcing exchange programmes and carrying out development projects.[13]

India has remained the light of Asia throughout the millennium. Moreover, argumentative traditions and pluralistic ethos have cemented our bondage. We are far ahead of China in democratic governance and domain of freedom. Nye analyzes that the country which has a better story only wins the race. 'India must remain the land of the better story'.[14] Having a blooming space for argumentative traditions and innovative ideas through the mass media, India really can attract the global audience or pull them through her stories compared to China in many respects.

Demographic dividend of India would foster the pace of its economic growth compared to China. The population of India which is 1.330 billion (as per the IDB estimation, 2009) is projected at 1.656 billion in 2025. Conversely, the population of China which is 1.173 billion (as per the IDB estimation, 2009) is projected at 1.395 billion in 2025. The population growth rate of China estimated for (2010-2015) is 0.6 percent while that of India is 1.3 percent for the same period. The working age group of population for China is projected at 70.6 percent in 2020 and 69.2 percent in 2025 while the corresponding figures for India are 67.0 percent and 69.2 percent respectively. However, India's working population (971 million) would overtake China (956 million) in 2028.[15] By this time, all the developed nations would experience negative growth of population thereby providing immense opportunities to the young Indian work force in the globalised economy.

However, it depends on how India takes advantage of this demographic dividend for economic development through skill formation, productive employment, innovative entrepreneurship, social sector management and corporate governance. The ageing population of India above 65+ was 5.3 percent in 2010 as contrast to China which stood at 8.6 percent. This trend in China would further gain momentum in the decades of thirties and forties.

The estimated figures for India in this category would be 10.2 percent in 2035 as against 21.0 percent for China.[16] The large chunk of ageing population in China will restrict the supply side of labour force adversely affecting the prospects of economic growth. However, the success story of Chinese planners lies how far they apply economic wisdom to handle the anticipated demographic drag to retain the tempo of economic growth in future.

Diversified diaspora provides favourable conditions to India compared to entrepreneurial diaspora of China. India has thirty million diaspora whereas China has fifty seven million diaspora.[17] Indian diaspora includes knowledge personnel, professionals, politicians and social workers. They are present across the globe which mainly includes UK, USA, Canada, Singapore, Fiji, Mauritius, Surinam, Middle East and East Africa. Chinese diaspora primarily consists of business entrepreneurs engaged in USA, Russia, Canada, Brazil, Peru, France, Singapore, South East Asia and Africa.[18] The mounting youth knowledge force of India would be a positive facet for further flow of remittance. Political diaspora would also prove highly beneficial while India would negotiate on economic and security issues at the bilateral or multilateral level.

India's geostrategic location in the Indian Ocean provides it adequate advantage over China. India is a 'credible naval power' in the region committed to regional peace, security and development.[19] The region banks upon the sea lines of communication for global trade and energy supply, and herein lies the significance of Strait of Malacca which is one of the busiest waterways (800 km) linking Andaman Sea in the Indian Ocean and South China Sea in the Pacific Ocean. It connects India, China, Japan, South Korea and ASEAN with the other economic groupings in a blooming maritime trade and energy ties.[20] China imports near about sixty five percent of its energy resources from West Asia and Africa through the Strait of Malacca. A major chunk of exports from China are also transhipped through this route. India vitally depends upon this transit for flourishing trade with the East. It rightly understood the strategic significance of the Strait and set up a naval base on the Andaman and Nicobar islands in the Bay of Bengal. It affirmed those Islands as India's gateway to the East, "to the Malacca Strait which is a 'throat channel' for our neighbouring Southeast Asia as well as Far East Asia.[21]

Noted Chinese intellectuals say that "India has repeatedly declared that it has security interests in the Malacca Strait, and its naval strategy stresses on maintaining its 'legitimate interests' from the Persian Gulf to the Malacca Strait".[22] They viewed that India's strategy was not aimed at containing China, but to flourish its regional influence to become a global power. So, India and China have no opposite interests in South East Asia, rather they have parallel objectives and can be equal partners to promote their mutual interests in the region.[23]

The economic prowess of both India and China has put them in gainful positions. They have sustained positive growth rate in spite of the global recession which destabilised the economies of many developed nations with negative growth rates succumbing to economic recessions. However, the economic growth model of India has an edge over China in long term perspective. The Indian economy is stimulated by robust entrepreneurship, energetic investment culture and strong financial system. India is integrated into the international market in an enhanced manner as compared to China. Yet, the Chinese academia ascribed certain reasons that might influence the growth story of India creating 'its own set of problems'. They viewed that 'compared with China's "authoritarian model", India's "democratic model" has its own weakness and has proved to be a drag on its rise and development'.[24]

A study of the above variables indicated that both India and China have enough competencies to steer the engine of the 21st century world. However, it is derived that India has many plus points against China. To cite one of such views:

> As the two growing powers of Asia sort out their places in their continent and the world, India has a comparative advantage over China that it does not always exploit: its status as the globe's largest democracy. For a while, when China was growing economically much faster than India, this advantage was not so obvious; you could conclude that democracy was too messy to allow rapid development. But India's pace of growth has picked up dramatically in the past decade, and it now can offer a model to similar Asian countries-themselves increasingly democratic-of growth and a humane government complementing each other.[25]

Cross Border Trade and Connectivity: A Tool for Regional Economic Integration

International trade has assumed immense significance vindicating the quintessence of mercantilist philosophy in global economic relations. The terra firma of WTO (World Trade Organisation) agreement is unfettered international trade harping on open border as well as free trade, thereby making the spatial domain of territory redundant in the twenty first century. The integration of India and China into the global economy, their competitiveness as well as engagement with major trading partners also brought a phenomenal increase in the volume of trade.[26] The bilateral trade which was US$ 2.92 billion in 2000 shot up to US$ 61.7 billion in 2010.[27] The trade boom continued and rose to US$75.45 billion (exports amounting 17.90 billion and imports amounting US$ 57.55 billion) in 2011-2012.[28] Even it is projected that the two way trade would touch US$ 100 billion mark by 2015.[29] No doubt, the bilateral trade made a quantum jump within a decade, even though India underwent adverse balance of payment with China during this period. So, India has to usher several measures to increase its exports for bringing parity with China in bilateral trade.

Cross border trade and connectivity which emerged as an important instrument of regional economic integration in the recent past has propelled India and China to grab the opportunities to expand their trade relations. As an upshot, they accorded priority to cross border trade and signed Memorandum of Understanding (MOU) at Beijing on 23 June 2003 to expand their trade basket. India agreed to declare Changgu of Sikkim being the border trade market place and China agreed to declare Reniqinggang of the Tibet Autonomous Region being the border trade market place. They also decided to operate Nathula as the entry and exit point for cross border trade.[30]

India was cognizant that all the regions have tremendous potentialities in geographical sense and its dividends should be reaped by the people through direct and participative way. It viewed the geo-economic importance of Eastern sector as the link between East and South East Asia in an era of regional and global co-operation. In this context, Eastern sector could bring India's economic integration with the East. Located in the North East of India, Arunachal Pradesh shares international border with Bhutan, China and Myanmar. The trading points could be developed at Kibithoo of Anjaw, Bumla and Kenzamane (Zeminthang) of Tawang, Gelling (Kepangla Pass) of Upper Siang, Mechuka (Lolla pass) and Monigong (Dumla pass) of West Siang districts of Arunachal Pradesh along Indo-China border and possibly other trading points with Bhutan and Myanmar as well for regional economic integration.[31] But the thrust for this lies how they revive the old Stilwell road involving all the stakeholders in the region.

Table 12.1: Cross Border Trading Points in Arunachal Pradesh

Country	*State*	*District*	*Trading Point*	*Border*
India	Arunachal Pradesh	Anjaw	Kibithoo	India-China Border
India	Arunachal Pradesh	Tawang	Bumla	India-China Border
India	Arunachal Pradesh	Tawang	Kenzamane (Zeminthang)	India-China Border
India	Arunachal Pradesh	Upper Siang	Gelling (Kepangla Pass)	India-China Border
India	Arunachal Pradesh	West Siang	Mechuka (Lolla Pass)	India-China Border
India	Arunachal Pradesh	West Siang	Monigong (Dumla Pass)	India-China Border

Source: Arunachal Pradesh, http://arunachalpradesh.nic.in/trade/html/introduction.htm Accessed on 24 January 2010.

Experts on border trade also suggest revamping the old Stilwell road to connect Ledo in Assam with Kunming in Yunnan province of China through Pangsau Pass in Arunachal Pradesh and Wauling at Mongya in Myanmar. They expect that the reopening of this strategic route would enhance the prospect of cross border trade with China as well as Myanmar. The connection of Stillwell road to the Asian High way project through Hukwang valley of Myanmar might expand economic co-operation and pave the way for formation of growth triangles or growth zones in future. However, its success depends upon the pragmatic considerations and the multilateral approach of India, Myanmar and China.[32]

Table 12.2: Stilwell Road (Ledo to Kunming)

Important Routes	*Distance in KM*	*Distance in Miles*
Ledo	0	0
Pangsau Pass	61	38
Tagap Hill	127	79
Sindbwiyang	165	103
Jambu-Bum	287	178
Warazup	304	189
Myitkyina	403	250
Bhamo	595	372
Namkham	707	439
Mong (Ledo-Burma)	749	465
Roads Junction		
Wanting	811	507
Lungling	896	560
Paoshan	1043	652
Yungpin	1208	755
Yunnanyi	1402	876
Tsuyung	1543	959
Kunming	1726	1079

Source: Stilwell Road: A Profile of Changlang District, http://changlang.nic.in/stilwell.html Accessed on 1 May 2012.

The Stilwell road which was built up during the World War II as an alternative conduit of transport to China is currently significant for cross border trade and regional economic integration in the context of India's Look East Policy and emerging free trade architecture with ASEAN. The road with a distance 1726 km starts from Ledo in Assam (India) and goes across Jairampur and Nampong and Pangsau pass in Arunachal Pradesh (India) and Shindbwiyang, Bhamo and Myitkyina in Kachin (Myanmar) linking Ledo-Burma roads junction through Yunnanyi and Tsuyung to the city of Kunming in Yunan in (China).The road covers 61 km in India,1033 km in Myanmar and 632 km in China.[33]

Myanmar Government assigned contract to Yunnan Construction Engineering Group of China to reconstruct 312 km road from Mytikyina in Myanmar to Pangsau pass in India-Myanmar border. The rebuilding of Mytikyina-Pangsau Pass would reduce the cost of transport near about 30 percent benefitting India, Myanmar and China for bilateral as well as multilateral trade.[34] India has pronounced its segment of Stilwell road as national highway 153 in October 2000 after holding a joint conference with Bangladesh, China and Myanmar in Kunming in 1999. China in order to augment its free trade regime with the ASEAN neighbours has renovated own segment of roadways through six lane Highways from the city of Kunming. Besides this, Beijing is also looking ahead to connect Kunming with Singapore through three trunk lines traversing Myanmar, Laos, Vietnam, Cambodia, Thailand and Malaysia, and is also optimistic to complete high speed rail network connecting Kunming with Singapore through the domestic railways of ASEAN by 2015.[35] In the event of these infrastructure are fully commissioned, goods from Singapore can directly reach Nampong, Ledo and other parts of North East India through Kunming Singapore Trunk Road or Kunming-Singapore railways and vice versa.[36]

The cross-border institutional machinery has offered opportunities for pragmatism as well as people centric moves as contrasted with mere territorial claims. However, the road map is to be prepared cautiously for the future. It should be two way traffic for ensuring growth and development in the region. Indian exports should sufficiently balance the imports from China and other South-East Asian nations. Otherwise, Arunachal Pradesh would be a dumping ground for the foreign products and it would adversely affect India's economic interest in the long term perspective. While envisioning cross border policies, Arunachal Pradesh should not be treated as a mere bridge; rather enough opportunities should be created for its contribution to the export basket of our country. But it would remain a wishful thinking only, until institutional reforms are made in Arunachal Pradesh. On the other, we should also be very cautious not to hamper the interest or the security of our country at any point of time in carrying out this project for cross-border economic integration.

Chinese Assertions over Arunachal Pradesh: India's Response

The recent Chinese assertions over Arunachal Pradesh might affect the bonhomie in cross border integration raising controversies between India and China. Chinese claim is neither substantiated by history nor by any other factor. People of the state are deeply interwoven with the socio-cultural mosaic and political landscape of India and it is an inseparable part of Indian Union. The historical records and the works substantiate Eastern sector being integral part of India. The British war Office which published the maps in 1907 illustrated the Eastern sector lying within Indian Territory.[37] The works of Francis Younghusband on 'India and Tibet' as well as Charles Bells on 'Tibet: Past and Present' clearly marked the Tribal area within Indian territory. The border was brought into line applying the watershed principle as generally practised in mountainous terrain after giving due consideration to historical, ethnic and strategic factors. The Shimla Agreement (1914) did not create a new boundary; it only formally delineated 'the natural, customary, traditional boundary in this sector.' During the Sino-Indian border conflict in 1962, China unilaterally made cease-fire and withdrew beyond the McMahon line which confirms India's North East Frontier along the McMahon Line.[38] The Chinese withdrawal legitimised and vindicated McMahon line as the international boundary between India and China. Notwithstanding this, Beijing's offensive statements beginning with Ambassador Sun Yuxi's claim over Arunachal Pradesh in November 2006 and then refutation of Chinese visa to an IAS officer in May 2007 reminded the days of Chinese belligerence in the sixties.[39] As a result, India cancelled the tour of entire batch of IAS officers to China.[40] China objected to the visit of Prime Minister Manmohan Singh to Arunachal Pradesh in 2009. India sharply reacted to it and affirmed that Arunachal Pradesh is an integral part of the country.[41] In the subsequent years, China blocked US $60 million Asian Development Bank project for Arunachal Pradesh citing that it could not approve the proposal because it lies in 'disputed territory.' India responded to the Chinese opposition telling to the ADB that 'there's no question of removing the Arunachal project from the plan'. Further, it reiterated that 'ADB cannot allow its forum for bilateral issues and link these to its lending policies'.[42] Recently, China also objected to Defence Minister A.K. Antony's visit to Arunachal Pradesh for taking part in the twenty five years of its Statehood Day on February 20, 2012. Antony criticised such Chinese opposition and termed them as the "most objectionable". He further said "Like Jammu and Kashmir, Arunachal Pradesh is an integral part of India and as Defence Minister he has both right and duty to visit the state and all other Border States".[43]

What could be the plausible factors for such assertions? Of course, the academia and the foreign policy watchers view such Chinese assertions from several perspectives.

One of the scholars of Chinese Institute of International Studies raised the point that India and China have not resorted to any armed conflict or border skirmish even though 'some media has played up such noises of China's invasions into India's territory dozens or hundreds of times'.[44] Since the global power stratagem is shifting from the West to the East in the 21st century, it may be analysed that Chinese threat perception is artificially created by the corporate driven media empire to prolong Western hegemony in the contemporary international relations as a sort of manufactured consent in the Chomskian epistemological traditions. Thus, the western world confronting with the challenges of economic recession seek a detour out of the impasse and explore all plausible options such as investment in the defence sectors and sale of arms to the Asian countries for their resurgence. So, any overstated hype of Chinese threat or exaggerated projection may convert Asia into a theatre of War in future. So, interdependence and convergence of interest can only replace such propaganda.

Chinese assertion is interpreted to counter growing Indo-US cooperation in the post cold war international politics in which the foreign policy watchers of Beijing consider India as a bulwark against the rise of China in the 21st century. But such contemplations are not based on ground realities. Rather, Indo-USA strategic partnership intends on securing India's energy security and economic development while focussing on cross-border integration, peace, stability and prosperity in the region.

Chinese assertion is accentuated owing to its suspicion on the role of Tibetans and Head of the Tibetan Government in Exile, His Holiness Dalai

Lama in India. However, India has made it clear that Tibet is an integral part of China and Dalai Lama is an Honoured Guest of India. India's External Affairs Minister S.M. Krishna said "The Indian position has been stated repeatedly and categorically. Dalai Lama is an honoured guest, a spiritual leader who is held as such by millions and we don't encourage anyone to get into political activities which will concern the relationship between the two sides. We have made it abundantly clear that Tibet is a part of China".[45] So, China should accept India's declared position on Tibet and repose confidence upon New Delhi for peaceful resolution of the bilateral issues.

Chinese assertion is also accounted to respond to the rise of India in the present-day world. India has occupied a major space in the global economy and recognised as a powerful nation with immense potentialities in many fields. Besides, India's Look East Policy has brought huge dividends reinforcing bilateral ties with the neighbourhood of South East Asia. Beijing apprehends that India's spatial expansion in economic and strategic domains might shrink Chinese spatial domain. However, it is well acknowledged that New Delhi's growing economic and diplomatic engagement with the South East and East Asia is not aimed at containing China, rather is a fall out of the process globalisation to secure growth, equity and development in the present day world.

Chinese posture over Arunachal Pradesh is also interpreted in terms of Beijing's envy for Two H (Hydrocarbon and Hydro Power) potential of Arunachal Pradesh. India has huge deposit of shale oil in Arunachal Pradesh and other states of North-East India. It is assumed that the region has the capacity to produce 140 million tonnes per annum for near about a century and can meet the growing energy demands of India and eventually spinning it into a net oil exporter. With the onset of horizontal drilling or the new technology otherwise termed as shale gas "fracking", the exploration of oil and gas in Arunachal Pradesh has become a ground reality.[46] Beijing is making similar claims on South China Sea due to its enormous oil deposits.[47] Since China would emerge as the biggest oil importer of the world in the coming decades, foreign policy watchers envisage that it might persist assertive attitude to tap the oil resources of the region. On the other, it is envisaged that China is also jealous of immense hydro power potentials (approximately 50,000 megawatt) of Arunachal Pradesh which is being tapped by India for country's growing energy requirements. Thus, it is imperative that any kind of provocation for encircling this region would foment trouble and would call for strong response from India to deter any threat.

The Chinese assertion over Arunachal is totally unjustified and at the same time it is not in conformity with the international law and tenets of international diplomacy. Nevertheless, India and China displayed their political acumen and pragmatism to resolve the boundary issue through 'Guiding Principles and political parameters 'agreed between them in 2005'.[48] The sustained dialogues could bring a new era or what could be termed by the Indian strategic thinkers as 'shift from the territorial imperative to political imperative".[49] Conversely, the Chinese think-tank was also quite optimistic and viewed the agreement as a great landmark to settle the border row between the two neighbors.[50] Further, India and China have also rejuvenated their positive attitude in pronouncing their respect to the Line of Actual Control and have agreed to maintain peace and tranquillity in the border areas for reinforcing mutual trust and security to resolve the Boundary Question at an early date as well as to build the 'India-China Strategic and Cooperative Partnership for Peace and Prosperity in the days ahead'.[51]

Thus, the revival of India China bhai-bhai spirit hinges on how effectively they deal with the bilateral issues. What is apparent here is that both India and China have resorted to sustained border negotiation mechanisms as well as confidence building measures to resolve the boundary row to generate an ambience of peace and stability in the region. Moreover, they have to tap their resources to the maximum possible extent to reap in the dividends of peace and development in Asia and the world. As we comprehend, the success of China neither lies in assertions nor in territorial conflagrations, but rests on peace and amity for future generations. To end the discussion with the words of Deng Xiaoping "Only when China and India develop well, can one claim that the century of Asia has come. If China and India strengthen cooperation, Asian unity, stability and prosperity will be very hopeful; the world will be in peace and make more progress".[52]

NOTES AND REFERENCES

1. J. Bandyopadhyaya, *The Making of India's Foreign Policy*, Allied Publishers, New Delhi, 1987, pp.4-5.
2. V.P. Dutt, *India's Foreign Policy*, National Book Trust, New Delhi, 2007, p.6.
3. "Panchsheel", External Publicity Division, Ministry of External Affairs, Government of India, New Delhi, accessed at http://meaIndia.nic.in/staticfile/meapublication/panchsheel.pdf, accessed on February 25, 2012.

4. *Ibid.*
5. "India-China Bilateral Relations", Ministry of External Affairs, Government of India, New Delhi, accessed at http://meaIndia.nic.in/meaxpsite/foreignrelation/china.pdf, accessed on February 26, 2012.
6. Jajati K. Pattnaik, "A Critique of Neo-liberal Development and Alternatives," Mainstream, vol. 46, no. 26 June, 2008, p.15.
7. See http://www.goldmansachs.com/our-thinking/brics/brics-reports-pdfs/ten-things-India.pdf, accessed on April 19, 2012. Also see C. Raja Mohan, "Indian Foreign Policy", World Focus, vol.27, no.11&12, November-December 2007.pp.392-93.
8. Harsh V. Pant, "Indian Foreign Policy and China", Strategic Analysis, Vol.30, No.4, October-December 2006, p.260.
9. Steve Jones, accessed at http://usforeignpolicy.about.com/od/introtoforeignpolicy/a/Soft-Power-In-U-S-Foreign- Policy.htm, accessed on April 14, 2012.
10. Shashi Tharoor, "Indian strategic Power: Soft," accessed at http://www.huffingtonpost.com/shashi-tharoor/Indian-strategic-power-so_b_207785.html, accessed on April 16, 2012.
11. *Ibid.*
12. Rosita Dellios and R. James Ferguson, "Sino-Indian Soft Power in a Regional Context," Culture Mandala: Bulletin of the Centre for East-West Culture and Economic Studies, Vol. 9, no. 2, September-December 2011, accessed at http://www.international-relations.com/CM2011/Sino-Indian-Soft-Power-2011.pdf, accessed on May 7, 2012.
13. *Ibid.*
14. Tharoor, n.10.
15. Charles Wolf, Jr., Siddhartha Dalal, Julie DaVanzoEric V. Larson, Alisher Akhmedjonov, Harun Dogo,Meilinda Huang & Silvia Montoya, "India and China, 2025: A comparative Assessment", National Defence Research Institute, Rand Corporation accessed at http://www.rand.org/content/dam/rand/pubs/monographs/2011/RAND_MG1009.pdf, accessed on March 30 2012.
16. *Ibid.*
17. "Promoting Investments from the Indian Diaspora: A New Beginning, Special Report," Overseas Indian Facilitation Centre, accessed at http://www.oifc.in/Uploads/MediaTypes/Documents/PromotingInvestmentsFromTheIndianDiaspora.pdf, accessed on February 29, 2012.
18. *Ibid.*
19. Gurpeet S. Khurana, "Cooperation among Maritime Security Forces: Imperatives for India and South East Asia," *Strategic Analysis*, vol. 29, no. 2, April-June 2005, p.29.
20. Centre for Strait of Malacca, accessed at http://www.mima.gov.my/index.php?option=com_content&view=article&id=85&Itemid=88, accessed on July 12, 2012.
21. Yang Dali & Zhao Hong, "The Rise of India: China's Perspectives and Responses, accessed at "http://www.daliyang.com/files/Yang_and_Zhao_The_Rise_of_India-china_s_perspectives_and_reponse.pdf, accessed on February 29, 2012.
22. *Ibid.*
23. *Ibid.*
24. *Ibid.*
25. Brahma Chellaney, *Asian Juggernaut*, Harper Collins Publishers India, New Delhi, 2007, p. 21.
26. Paola Subacchi, "China and India in Changing Global economic Order", January 2007, accessed at http://www.chathamhouse.org/sites/default/files/public/Research/International%20Economics/0107subacchi.pdf, accessed on August 20, 2012.

27. "India china Bilateral Relations", Embassy of India, Beijing, accessed at http://www.indianembassy.org.cn, accessed on February 26, 2012.
28. "India China Meet to Resolve Trade Matters, Strengthen Ties", *Business Standard,* September 24, 2012.
29. *Ibid.*
30. "Memorandum of Understanding between the Government of India and the Government of the People's Republic of China on Expanding Border Trade", (Appendix) cited in Chellaney, n. 25, pp. 320-21.
31. K. Alam, "The Prospect of Cross Country Border Trade of Arunachal Pradesh", in S Dutta, (ed.), *Cross Border Trade of North East India,* Hope India Publications, Haryana, 2002, pp.164-165. Also see, Jajati K Pattnaik, "Neo-Liberal Paradigm and Development in Arunachal Pradesh: A Vision for Future," Dialogue, January-March 2009, p.111.
32. *Ibid.*
33. "Stilwell Road: A Profile of Changlang District," accessed at http://changlang.nic.in/stilwell.html, accessed on May 1, 2012.
34. Sudha Ramachandran, "Stilwell Road to be Reborn", Asia Times, accessed at http://www.atimes.com/atimes/South_Asia/MA12Df03.html, accessed on May 2, 2012.
35. Ashiq Uz Zaman, "Stilwell Road: Connecting Future", Seven Sisters Post (Guwahati), May 15, 2012.
36. *Ibid.*
37. M.L. Bose, *History of Arunachal Pradesh,* Concept Publishing company, New Delhi, 1997, p.147.
38. *Ibid.*, pp.147-149.
39. P. Stobdan, "India's Tibet Policy," *World Focus,* vol. 27, nos. 11&12, November-December 2007, p. 422. For the statement of Chinese Ambassador, see http://www.rediff.com/news/2006/nov/14china, accessed on September 22, 2012.
40. Srikanth Kondapalli, "Eleventh Round of Border Talks: India-China border Dispute," World Focus, vol.28, no.11&12, November-December 2007, p.414.
41. See http://www.indianexpress.com/news/arunachal-is-an-integral-part-of-india-mea-to-china/52858, accessed on September 5, 2012.
42. See http://www.indianexpress.com/news/at-adb-beijing-blocks-indias-60m-project-for-arunachal/446709/, accessed on September 5, 2012.
43. See http://www.thehindu.com/news/national/article, accessed on August 22, 2012.
44. Xuecheng Liu, "Look beyond the Sino Indian Border Dispute," Presented at the Workshop on Revisit Sino-Indian Border Dispute, Westminster University, London, June 2010 , accessed at http://www.ciis.org.cn/english/2011-08/11/content_4401017.htm, accessed on March 30, 2012).
45. "Tibet a Part of China, Dalai Lama an Honoured Guest", accessed at http://www.ndtv.com/article/India/tibet-a-part-of-china-dalai-lama-an-honoured-guest-krishna-46209, accessed on August 30, 2012.
46. Swaminathan A. Aiyar, "Will China Eye Arunachal Pradesh's Shale Oil?" accessed at http://blogs.timesofindia.indiatimes.com/Swaminomics/entry/will-china-eye-arunachal-pradesh-s-shale-oil, accessed on June 14, 2013.
47. See http://blogs.timesofindia.indiatimes.com/Swaminomics/entry/will-china-eye-arunachal-pradesh-s-shale-oil, accessed on September 2, 2012.
48. *Ibid.*
49. C. Raja Mohan, "Soft Borders and Cooperative Frontiers: India's Changing Territorial Diplomacy towards Pakistan and China," *Strategic Analysis,* vol.31, no.1, January 2007,

p.13. Also see, India and China reached an agreement on the 'Political Parameters and Guiding principles for the settlement of the Boundary Question' in 2005 which inter alia mentioned 'a fair, reasonable and mutually acceptable solution to the boundary question through consultations on an equal footing'; 'meaningful and mutually acceptable adjustments to their respective positions on the boundary question to arrive a package settlement'; 'due consideration to each other's strategic and reasonable interests and the principle of mutual and equal security'; 'take into account; inter alia, historical evidence, national sentiments, practical difficulties and reasonable concerns and sensitivities of both sides, and the actual state of border areas'; 'the boundary should be along well-defined and easily identifiable natural geographical features to be mutually agreed upon'; 'safeguard due interests of their settled populations in the border areas in reaching a boundary settlement'; 'delineate the boundary utilising modern cartographic means and surveying practices and joint survey;" respect and observe the line of actual control and work together to maintain peace and tranquillity in the border areas pending an ultimate settlement of the boundary question.' Cited in Chellaney n.25, p.180.

50. Raja Mohan, n.49, p.15.
51. Liu, n.44.
52. "Bilateral Documents: India China Agreement on the Establishment of a Working Mechanism for Consultation and co-ordination on India-China Border Affairs," Ministry of External Affairs Library, Government of India, New Delhi, accessed at http://mealib.nic.in/?2010201218925, accessed on February 25, 2012.

Chapter 13

Sino-Indian Relations: Competition or Cooperation?

C. Joshua Thomas

Territorial dispute among the countries is one of the sources of international tensions and conflicts. The use of force in the establishment of claims is increasingly becoming a thing of the past and negotiations are chosen over war in coming into terms as the cost of war is too high for the nations compared to mutual accommodation of each other's interest.

Usually claims of a country over a territory is based on historically evolved relationship between them characterized by ethnic affinities, linguistic and cultural similarity, and administrative and governance linkages.

Chinese claim over Arunachal Pradesh is rested on the argument that China sees this territory as part of Tibet which she calls Southern Tibet. Thus, Chinese claim is not rested on any historical linkages between mainland China and the territory under Indian state of Arunachal Pradesh. It is in fact a derived claim. But did Tibet ever claim Arunachal Pradesh as her part?

In spite of the fact that Tibet had some sort of influence over Tawang Tract and the Tawang Monastery is the second largest centre of Tibetan Buddhism where Sixth Dalai Lama was born, Tibet ceded this area to British India by virtue of signing the Simla Accord in 1914. Till the annexation of Tibet by China in 1950, both India and Tibetan governments considered McMahon Line to be the border between them. Thus, in spite of the fact that China does not recognize the McMahon Line, one may argue, does she has any choice? While India has inherited the boundaries of British India, China has inherited the boundaries of Tibet. While India accepts the McMahon Line as her northeastern border, why does China refuse to accept the same. If Chinese plenipotentiary refused to sign the Simla Accord, how does it invalidate the Accord? It might be noted that Tibet had declared independence well before the Accord which was signed between the two independent entities—British India and Tibet. One may question as to why would the world accept Chinese historiography and refute the Tibetan historiography? Since China did not recognize Tibetan independence and hence refused to accept the McMahon Line, why did she expect others also to fall in line? If writing history of "others" in the light of the "self-image" is only imperial in nature, does China has any moral ground to criticize the McMahon Line as a colonial imposition?

In fact, neither Tibet was a part of modern China, nor Arunachal Pradesh was a part of modern India while they born in 1949 and 1947 respectively. Unlike Tibet, there was no state formation among the tribal communities living between "inner line" (north of Assam) and "outer line" (that roughly corresponds the McMahon Line) of British India. British did not bring these hill tribes under direct rule but had exercised some sort of indirect influence in order to desist them from raiding the plains of Assam. This vast tract of ungoverned frontier was brought under North East Frontier Agency (NEFA) and then rechristened as Arunachal Pradesh by India and brought under regular administration following the Chinese thrust towards Tibet. Following the Chinese occupation of Tibet, India immediately acknowledged and followed the forward policy to catch up the McMahon Line with the hope that China will also acknowledge her (India's) interest in Arunachal Pradesh. The rest of the sequence of events that led to 1962 war is well known and we do not intend to repeat the same.[1]

What is of our interest is the fact that neither China nor India has undisputable historical support in favour of their claims as far as Arunachal Pradesh is concerned. As a result, taking recourse to history will not lead them anywhere in settling the score. Instead, both the nations should adopt a pragmatic approach. As Tibet has already been integrated with the mainland China, and Arunachal Pradesh with mainland India, it is only pragmatic that China recognizes Arunachal Pradesh as an inseparable part of India and, in turn, India accepts Tibet as an inalienable part of China.

The Eastern Sector needs to be delinked from the Western Sector and an understanding between the two nations is to be reached to resolve the border dispute. As the McMahon Line roughly corresponds to Line of Actual Control (LAC), it is only prudent to demarcate the Sino-Indian border in the Eastern Sector along the LAC.

Unfortunately, the settlement of border dispute in the Eastern Sector is becoming complicated by each day with the Chinese behaving in a belligerent manner by way of hardening her stand on Arunachal Pradesh. Earlier China claimed only Tawang where Tibetan Buddhism has pronounced influence, but recently she started claiming the whole of Arunachal Pradesh. Further, China's objection to the visit of Indian Prime Minister and the Defence Minister to Arunachal Pradesh is a disturbing thing to the Indian leadership and more particularly for the people in the North-Eastern region. It has been widely reported as to how China has blocked Asian Development Bank assistance to Arunachal Pradesh, and how it has refused to provide visa to the officials from Arunachal Pradesh. Moreover, China has created a disturbing trend by the PLA's frequent intrusion into the Indian territory.

This act of Chinese belligerency has badly affected the relationship between the two civilizational neighbours and also slowly it has brought more tension among the other Asian countries. Although the cold war which existed between the United States and the former Soviet Union disappeared three decades ago, now a new cold war raises its monstrous head between India-China in a different way. In response to Chinese attempts to militarize Tibet, India is also mobilizing her war machine in the neighbourhood of the McMahon Line. This war-like posture among these two giants of Asia will certainly push both the countries competing with one another in every field and ultimately might push for war to settle their score. As both India and China are nuclear powers and if 1962 like war is repeated, there will be nuclear holocaust in Asia. Therefore, the border dispute is not only the concern of the people of India and China but also for a great concern for the countries in the world at large.

However, in spite of this confrontationist attitude, the two nations have also developed cooperative relationship in a number of areas. It might be noted that no incident of firing was recorded in any part of the Sino-Indian border for more than fifty years, since the border war of 1962. Whereas in case of India-Pakistan border, there has been frequent cross-firing, rampant violation of LOC and border skirmishes.

There has been a vast improvement in Sino-Indian bilateral economic relations. The bilateral trade has taken a great leap forward where China has become India's largest trade partner in the world. Bilateral investment in each other is on the rise. The space for mutual cooperation is expanding and the frequency of visits by head of the states between them has substantially increased. Besides economic relationship, both the countries are increasingly engaging each other in a wide spectrum of areas including defence training and cooperation.

It has been realized that war is not the solution but dialogue and continual talks at all levels is the only way to settle border dispute between India-China. Both the countries must make sincere efforts to eliminate differing perception about boundary dispute. The spirit of give and take[2] instead of stubbornness in their perception on boundary dispute needs to prevail. It is time to address the larger issues such as lifting millions of people from poverty, bridging the gap between the rich and poor, infrastructure development, investment and collaborating in areas like climate change, G-20, BRICS, etc. However, it has been seen widely that systemic misunderstanding is a major issue in Sino-Indian relations. Due to cultural differences, Indian elites hardly understand Chinese "codes of gestures" and as a result fail to interpret their implications for bilateral relations. The pronouncements of the Chinese statesmen and their actions often do not match. Many a times this happens due to mismatch between Chinese global strategic architecture and Sino-Indian bilateral relations. Thus, mutual distrust should be removed from both sides and for this closer interaction between them at all levels including the exchange of academic scholars, sports persons, journalists should be encouraged.

Although both countries agreed that there is 'enough space in Asia' for them to thrive, it is essential that certain long-term understanding on issues such as providing a level playing field in capital investments, high-technology acquisition, market explorations, contribution to expansion of infrastructure projects, counter-terrorism, curbing proliferation of weapons of mass destruction and avoiding costly arms race or outer space weaponisation. As both configure their national strategies for expanding inclusive economic growth, it is necessary that bilateral frictions are consciously avoided.[3] The earlier the border dispute between India and China is settled the better it will be for the peace, security and development of Asia and for the world. People both in India's Northeast and in China's Southwest earnestly desire a lasting solution should be found for the boundary dispute which will ultimately pave way for the Asian Century.[4]

Thus, in order to improve the Sino-Indian bilateral relations, statesmen in both countries need to weave the bilateral relations around the growing economic interdependence between the countries. The growth strategy in both the countries needs to be strongly rooted in bilateral complementarities rather than adversarial competition. Both, India and China need to shed the ideological preconceptions about each other. As both the countries are working for maximizing their respective national interests, there is no point for China to view India as an ally of the Western nations. Similarly, there is no point for India to see China as a communist ideologue that prefers to settle dispute using might rather than compromise. For this, the historical linkages and the cultural commonalities need to be highlighted as the basis for future relations rather than the spat in bilateral relations that took place in 1962. Together, China and India can reform the global order than trying to grow alone at the cost of the other. As it has aptly been said that India and China may not become best friends again but it can certainly be ensured that they become comfortable neighbours and neither harms the other directly or indirectly.

Further, it is worth to quote the observation by Brajesh Mishra, one of the influential security manager who acted as India's Special Representative: "From our point of view, we should be willing to make pragmatic compromises to fulfill the strategic objective of a comprehensive boundary settlement with China ...We must never allow sentiment to govern foreign policy issues or those relating to national security...Policy and diplomacy must be based on hard realities and not sentiments".[5]

It is only appropriate to mention that regional peace is the *sine qua non* for the development of both the nations. Neither the "peaceful rise" of China nor the "emergence of India" is possible in a conflict ridden environment. As a "benign power image" would facilitate China's ascendance to global power rather than a "belligerent image", she cannot afford to adopt a coercive border policy vis-à-vis India. If the frequent incursions by the PLA across the LAC is a deliberate policy to belittle India among the comity of nations in general and countries in Asia in particular as well as intending to send signals to the countries and peoples across the Himalayas that India is not in a position to defend them and hence it is better for them to switch over their loyalty towards China, then this arms twisting approach is certain to backfire as the nuclear weapons have equalized the "power gap", traditional war advantage of China over India, between them. If the incursions are meant to prove that India is militarily weak and hence China intends to settle the border rows in her own terms, this might lead India to hedge China by way of forging strategic alliances with forces inimical to China. In such an eventuality, instead of a good neighbor, China would have to live with a hostile neighbour keeping her backyard unprotected. If China is to rise as a global power, she has to come to terms with India. Otherwise, the convergence of interests between existing superpower and India might create an environment to contain China within Asia *a la* Chinese strategy to contain India within South Asia where Pakistan plays the second fiddle.

Thus, while adversarial relationship will harm the interest of both the nations, cooperative relationship between them is pregnant with immense possibilities. As one of the famous Indian business tycoons, Ratan Tata, once remarked, "China is the factory of the world; India can be the knowledge center of this region...If we orient ourselves to working together, we could be a formidable force of two nations".[6] Can the political masters in both the nations adopt a similar professional approach to mend the boundary disputes between them?

NOTES & REFERENCES

1. Boundary issues have always occupied a central focus in the relations between India and China. Thus, border issue is not only complex, but also very complicated. Each side is fully cognizant of the other's stand, both have agreed to maintain peace and tranquility in the border areas pending final solution and the special representative frameworks—this appears to be the point at which matters stand. See, Alka Acharya, "India-China Relations: Towards a 'Shared Vision'" in *Economic & Political Weekly,* January 26, 2008, pp. 10-13. A large number of books. monographs, articles have appeared on the Sino-Indian border dispute and some of the following may be useful reference, A.G. Noorani, *India-China Boundary Problem, 1846-1947: History and Diplomacy,* Oxford University Press, New Delhi, 2011; J.P. Dalvi, *Himalayan Blunder: The Curtain Raiser to the Sino-Indian War of 1962,* Natraj Publishers, Dehra Dun, 2010; *China Report, Special Issue on Revisiting the China-India Border Dispute,* Editor Dibyesh Anand, Sage Publication, New Delhi, vol.47, no.2, May 2011; A.G. Noorani, "The Truth About 1962—It is time for an honest retrospect on how a border problem was allowed to grow into a dispute and trigger an unnecessary war with China," in *Frontline,* Chennai, November 30, 2012, pp.4-20; Neville Maxwell, *India's China War,* Dehradun, Nataraj Publishers, 2010 (Reprint); Neville Maxwell, "The Sino-Indian Border Dispute Reconsidered", *Economic & Political Weekly*, vol. 34, issue no. 15, April 10, 1999, pp. 905-18; Neville Maxwell, "Why the Sino-Indian Border Dispute is Still Unresolved after 50 years: A Recapitulation", in *China Report*, vol. 47, no. 2, May 2011, pp. 71-82.

2. While inaugurating the *National Seminar on Voices from the Border: India's Response to Chinese Claim on Arunachal Pradesh* organized by the Indian Council of Social Science Research, North-Eastern Regional Centre, Shillong in collaboration with the Rajiv Gandhi University at Itanagar on 8th March 2012 General J.J. Singh (Retired), Governor of Arunachal Pradesh, unequivocally said: "some give and take is necessary for solving the India-China border dispute." It cannot be denied that for the first time an Indian top official has come out with such categorical views which is being looked upon as a departure from official positions adopted by New Delhi so far against making any compromise on the boundary problem with China. See, "China: India is Signaling Border 'Concessions', Feel Analysts", D.S. Rajan, C3S paper no.981 dated May 7, 2012 (http://www.c3sindia.org/india/2907 accessed on 29 May 2012.
3. Srikanth Kondapalli, "Enough Space in Asia", in *India-China Ties 60 Years 60 Thoughts,* published by the Embassy of India, Beijing, China, p. 81.
4. It was the first visit by an Indian Prime Minister to China since 1954 and it reciprocated, after a gap of nearly 28 years, Premier Zhou En-lai's 1960 visit. Rajiv Gandhi's discussions with Chinese leaders significantly enhanced mutual confidence and understanding between both sides. As a result of this a Joint Working Group was formed for negotiations on the boundary issue and for exploring ways of maintaining peace and tranquility along the Line of Actual Control in the border areas. Another Working Group was set up to promote trade and investment. Agreements were signed on cooperation in cultural exchanges, on science and technology and on civil aviation. In short, steps were taken to promote all-round bilateral cooperation and to maintain a tension-free Line of Actual Control while the two sides continued to seek a peaceful solution to the border issue. See, Biswaranjan Mohanty, *Foreign Policy of India in the 21st Century* by New Century Publications, New Delhi, pp. 287-93.
5. It is interesting to note from the address which Brajesh Mishra, India's former Ambassador to China & the National Security Advisor, delivered at a seminar organized by the ORF at Calcutta during early 2009. He quoted what Li Peng, the then Chairman of the National Peoples' Congress in one of his public interactions in Delhi, what was lacking in India-China relations was trust. Mutual distrust has stalled the boundary settlement all these years. See, S.D. Muni & Suranjan Das (edited) *India and China: The Next Decade,* Rupa & Co. in association with Observer Research Foundation, New Delhi, pp. 119–120.
6. Zoher Aboolcharim in his write up on "The Chindian Century" in *Time*, Vol. 178, No.20, November 21, 2011, pp. 38-40, argues, "With so many of the world's economics in tatters, the combined might of China and India could spearhead global growth in the coming decades. Are they up to the job?"

Index